101 Easy Homemade Products

FOR YOUR SKIN, HEALTH & HOME

A NERDY FARM WIFE'S
ALL-NATURAL DIY PROJECTS USING
COMMONLY FOUND HERBS,
FLOWERS & OTHER PLANTS

Jan Berry

FOUNDER OF THE BLOG THE NERDY FARM WIFE

PAGE STREET
PUBLISHING CO.

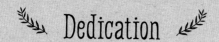

Dedication

To my husband and children, who are my best friends and biggest fans. Thank you for always cheering me on and being patient while "The Book" consumed our lives for a season. Now that it's done, I promise more lazy creek days and homemade ice cream, and less computer time and baked chicken (again?!) for supper.

PAGE STREET
PUBLISHING CO.

Copyright © 2016 Jan Berry

First published in 2016 by
Page Street Publishing Co.
27 Congress Street, Suite 103
Salem, MA 01970
www.pagestreetpublishing.com

Distributed by Macmillan, sales in Canada by The Canadian Manda Group.

19   18   17   16   1   2   3   4   5

ISBN-13: 978-1-62414-201-7
ISBN-10: 1-62414-201-X

Library of Congress Control Number: 2015949962

Cover and book design by Page Street Publishing Co.
Photography by Jan Berry

Printed and bound in China

Contents

Introduction

Have you ever surveyed your patch of mint or lemon balm and wondered how that one tiny plant you bought in a fit of spring fever five years ago managed to take over half of your flower beds?

I sure have.

In spite of my jungle of a garden, I still can't resist buying or growing new varieties of flowers and herbs as I discover them. Rather than give up my compulsion, I've made it my mission to see how creative I can get in using those plants that surround me.

My goal in writing this book is to share that passion and give you a tiny taste of the possibilities that are growing right around you as well.

I want to show you how to grab a rose from your garden, a handful of dandelions from your backyard or a bunch of basil from your local farmer's market, and make something beautiful, useful and good for you, your family and your home.

Because I live on a tight budget and Internet shipping costs a small fortune, it's important to me to use as many ingredients as I can source locally. When you live in rural America like I do, the store options are slim, but I'm still able to find most of my ingredients within a 30-mile (48-km) radius. For the things that do have to be ordered online, I've listed a few of my favorite vendors in the resource section in the back of this book.

I try to keep my recipes and instructions pretty straightforward, but if you run into a question or problem, please email me via my website's contact page, and I'll be happy to help.

Now if you're ready to make some fun stuff with me, turn the page and let's get started!

Getting Started Making Natural, Homemade Products

Common Herbs & Flowers & Their Benefits

Our gardens and backyards are filled with flowers, herbs and weeds that have the potential to provide many fun and useful products for home, health and beauty. If you can safely eat a plant, there's a good chance that it can be used in other interesting ways as well.

Although I've listed details about the ones specifically used to make the projects in this book, this isn't an all-inclusive list of plants with benefits. Explore the Internet, your library and local bookstore to find articles and books about herbs and edible flowers that grow in your locality. Some common plants, such as roses and basil, are easily recognizable, but always be certain of the identification of what you're harvesting before use.

Basil has anti-inflammatory, antioxidant, antibacterial and tick-repelling properties. Taken orally, it has an analgesic (pain relieving) affect on chronic pain conditions and makes a good expectorant in cough syrups. Basil opens up the sinuses, helps headaches, can be used in baths for stress or pain, as a toner for acne, rubbed on bug bites, incorporated in a salve for joint aches and has even been shown in one study to be effective in an antiaging cream. In short, basil is not just for pesto!

→ Basil & Rose Kombucha Toner—page 46

→ Basil & Lime Lip Balm—page 126

→ Create Your Own Vinegar Hair Rinse—page 150

→ Catnip & Basil Insect Repellant Spray—page 191

→ Basil Mint Sore Throat Spray—page 201

Calendula is a well-loved and often used flower that's included in many skin care recipes. It's a classic addition to diaper creams for babies, due to its anti-inflammatory, antibacterial and skin healing properties. It may help conditions such as eczema, is a lymphatic (helps relieve congested lymph nodes), good for sore throats and swollen tonsils, helps skin regenerate and is used in formulations to reduce the swelling and appearance of varicose veins. The tea can be used as an antiseptic wound wash. It should not be used internally by pregnant women.

→ Calendula Whipped Coconut Oil—page 71

→ Calendula Whipped Coconut Butter—page 72

→ Basic Calendula Lotion—page 81

→ Calendula Spice Fizzing Bath Salts—page 101

→ Calendula Spice & Honey Cleansing Scrub—page 113

→ Dry Shampoo for Light Hair Tones—page 147

→ Carrot & Calendula Soap—page 182

→ Bug Bite Powder—page 197

→ Itchy Skin Rinse—page 234

→ All-Purpose Animal Salve—page 237

Catnip is a cooling and drying herb. It repels mosquitoes and flies, is a mild analgesic (pain reliever), calms the nerves so a person can rest, is added to bath soaks to relieve stress and can be used in a hair rinse for dandruff. As a tea it may help relieve colds, coughs, upset stomach, nausea, toothache and headache.

→ Create Your Own Vinegar Hair Rinse—page 150

→ Catnip & Basil Insect Repellant Spray—page 191

Chamomile is antibacterial, antifungal, antiseptic and anti-inflammatory. Chamomile has been shown to have a mild cortisone-like effect and is often used in lotions, creams, salves and other products to help relieve rashes, irritated or red skin and eczema.

- Chamomile Honey Face Wash—page 36
- Honey & Chamomile Cream—page 91
- Calming Bath Soak—page 98
- Lavender Sleepy Time Bath Tea—page 104
- Lemon Chamomile Bath Melts—page 112
- Chamomile Brown Sugar Scrub Cubes—page 120
- Chamomile Lip Scrub—page 135
- Chamomile "Almost Castile" Soap—page 162
- Chamomile Calming Syrup—page 209

Cornflower is also called Bachelor Button. The flower extract is used as a skin conditioner and astringent. The petals add color to teas or bath soaks, and contain anti-inflammatory properties. A finely filtered tea can be used to soothe eye irritation and reduce puffiness.

- Lavender Blue Mask—page 51

Daisy is a common roadside weed found in many places. The flowers can be used for coughs and bronchitis. Common daisies were known in the past as a traditional wound herb for bruises, broken bones, eczema, inflammation and infection, and in more recent years have been the subject of a study that scientifically verified their wound-healing abilities.

- Daisy Vanilla Lip Balm—page 129

Dandelion may be vilified by those who seek a perfectly green lawn each spring, but it is an important plant in a multitude of beneficial ways. The flowers are among the first food sources for bees. They are also a good source of lecithin, and when infused in oil and turned into salves, lotions and creams, act as a mild analgesic (pain reliever) and healing agent for painful, chapped skin. The plant tincture stimulates the liver and has been known to clear acne and eczema when taken internally over time. It has also been studied for its cancer-fighting potential. Traditionally, dandelion sap has been used to treat microbial or fungal skin infections along with acne and warts.

- Dandelion Thyme Vinegar Toner & Tonic—page 45
- Dandelion Cuticle Balm—page 62
- Dandelion Body Butter—page 67
- Floral Salt Foot Scrub Bars—page 119

(continued)

Dianthus is an ornamental bedding plant, with flowers in shades of white, pink and red and are also called "pinks." The edible flowers can be used as a garnish, but I primarily use them in body care recipes as a natural colorant for bath salts and sugar scrubs.

Elder flowers help heal wounds and have been used for generations as an aid to obtaining a beautiful complexion. The berries of this shrub are a proven treatment for influenza.

Forsythia is a common, bright yellow flowering shrub whose blooms are among the first signs of spring each year. While the autumn fruits are traditionally the plant part used as medicine, the flowers can be utilized in a similar, milder-acting manner. Forsythia is cooling, anti-inflammatory and combines splendidly with honeysuckle to fight viruses. The flowers can also be used in preparations for acne or skin flare-ups.

Hollyhock is a cousin to the herb marsh mallow and shares similar soothing, cooling and anti-inflammatory properties. The flowers and leaves can be infused in oil to make salves and creams.

Lavender is one of the most loved herbs around. The sweet-scented plant is antibacterial, antifungal, anti-inflammatory, acts to regenerate skin, soothes inflammation, speeds up wound healing, fights infection, repels flies, fleas and moths and freshens laundry. Lavender can be incorporated in a multitude of products for health and home, including salves, creams, lotions, soaps, cleaners and more. While the flowers are most commonly used, the leaves can be utilized in many recipes as well.

Lemon Balm is a mild stress reliever, uplifts mood and has a marked antiviral effect, especially against herpes viruses, making it ideal for including in lip balms and salves for cold sores.

Lemongrass is a powerhouse of beneficial properties. It's anti-amebic and antibacterial, a decoction of the stalk acts as an antidiarrheal, the infused oil is antifungal, the fresh leaves are antifebrile (a fever reducer), a tea of dried leaves is anti-inflammatory and the essential oil is antimalarial. All that, and it smells wonderful, too!

Mint is cooling and pain relieving. It can help ease stomachache, indigestion, headache, nausea and sore muscles. It's useful in salves for cooling itchy or inflamed skin conditions. While peppermint and spearmint are most commonly used, you can also use orange mint, pineapple mint, apple mint, chocolate mint and other such varieties.

(continued)

- Mint Cocoa Body Butter—page 68

- Aloe Mint After-Sun Lotion—page 82

- Garden Herbs Bath Soak—page 97

- Sore Muscle Bath Bags—page 103

- Energizing Rosemary Mint Bath Tea—page 104

- Whipped Spearmint Scrub Butter—page 116

- Classic Peppermint Lip Balm—page 126

- Chocolate Mint Lip Balm—page 126

- Mint Lip Scrub—page 136

- Cucumber Mint Soap—page 184

- Basil Mint Sore Throat Spray—page 201

- Fresh Mint Wall Wash—page 227

- Peppermint & Parsley Fresh-Breath Dog Treat—page 238

Nettle is anti-inflammatory, astringent, healing, antibacterial, antimicrobial, nutritious and can be used externally as a treatment for dandruff and acne. It's included in many hair care formulations to improve scalp circulation and to stimulate hair growth.

- Nettle, Coconut & Honey Hair Mask—page 142

- Herbal Dry Shampoo for Dark Hair Tones—page 147

- Create Your Own Vinegar Hair Rinse—page 150

- Nettle & Coconut Oil Vitamin Treats—page 241

Oregano is powerful against bacteria and fungus, helps fight upper respiratory infections and contains several vitamins, minerals and potent antioxidants. It's a great addition to cold care remedies.

- Oregano Oxymel—page 202

- Four Thieves Vinegar Spray—page 220

Parsley is best known as a breath freshener. It's nutritious and high in vitamins A, C and K, helps eliminate the uric acid that causes gout and may be beneficial to animals with arthritis.

- Peppermint & Parsley Fresh-Breath Dog Treat—page 238

Peony is an old-fashioned garden flower used in this book as a natural colorant for scrubs and bath salts. Use dark pink or red peonies; the palest pink flowers don't work as well.

➤ Peony & Orange Sugar Scrub—page 115

➤ Floral Salt Foot Scrub Bars—page 119

Pine is high in vitamin C and antioxidants. The resin is antibacterial and helpful for sore, stiff joints and rheumatism. Pine is very warming and increases circulation.

➤ Peppermint Pine Headache Salve—page 60

➤ Garden Herbs Bath Soak—page 97

➤ Sore Muscle Bath Bags—page 103

➤ Orange Pine Floor Cleaner—page 223

Plantain is a common weed found in many backyards and driveways. It cools, soothes and moistens and is one of the best herbs for skin irritations, cuts, bug bites and scrapes. For in-field first aid, you can simply grab a leaf from your yard, pulverize it by chewing on it a few seconds, then place it directly on the irritation for relief. Plantain, the green leafy weed, should not be confused with plantain fruit. Plantain makes a very nice infused oil for soaps, salves and lip balms.

➤ Garden Herbs Bath Soak—page 97

➤ Dandelion Plantain Chapped Lip Treatment—page 129

➤ All-Purpose Animal Salve—page 237

Rose is a gentle remedy for inflammation. It's astringent, soothing, cools hot flashes, can be mixed with honey to make a soothing throat syrup and is an excellent addition to skin care recipes. The scent of rose uplifts the spirits and gladdens the heart.

➤ Honey, Rose & Oat Face Cleanser—page 35

➤ Basil & Rose Kombucha Toner—page 46

➤ Rose Pink Face Mask—page 51

➤ Regenerating Rose Balm—page 59

➤ Cocoa Rose Lotion Bars—page 77

➤ Rose Face Cream—page 86

➤ Fizzy Rose Lemonade Soak—page 102

➤ Lavender Sleepy Time Bath Tea—page 104

➤ Vanilla Rose Bath Melts—page 110

➤ Floral Salt Foot Scrub Bars—page 119

(continued)

Rosemary increases circulation, making it wonderful for use in sore muscle salves and recipes for healthier scalp and hair growth. Just a whiff of rosemary has been shown to increase concentration and focus.

Sage is warming and drying. It reduces sweating and is a good antimicrobial for sore throat. Since it's such a drying herb, nursing mothers should not ingest more than normal culinary use, or it may negatively affect milk supply.

Sunflowers have skin-soothing, anti-inflammatory properties and are used in formulations for shiny hair.

Thyme is a potent disinfectant, making it a good choice for treating cuts, scrapes and sore throats. It's also been shown to be highly effective against the bacteria that cause acne.

- ➤ Dandelion Thyme Vinegar Toner & Tonic—page 45
- ➤ Thyme & Raw Honey Mask—page 48
- ➤ Grapeseed & Thyme Lotion (for Oily Skin)—page 85
- ➤ Garden Herbs Bath Soak—page 97
- ➤ Thyme Flaky Scalp Spray—page 143
- ➤ Thyme & Witch Hazel Clear Skin Facial Bar—page 171
- ➤ Lemon Thyme Dusting Spray—page 214
- ➤ Four Thieves Vinegar Spray—page 220

Violets are high in vitamins A and C. They're soothing and cooling, help relieve swollen or congested lymph glands and are good for a dry cough and sore throat. Traditionally, violet leaves and flowers have been used in poultices, salves and massage oils for fibrocystic breasts. They're also reputed to ease the pain of headache.

- ➤ Violet Flower Cleanser—page 39
- ➤ Violet-Infused Aloe—page 47
- ➤ Violet Leaf Lotion Bars—page 76
- ➤ Violet & Aloe Moisturizing Cream—page 92
- ➤ Garden Herbs Bath Soak—page 97
- ➤ Floral Salt Foot Scrub Bars—page 119
- ➤ Create Your Own Vinegar Hair Rinse—page 150
- ➤ Violet Flower Sore Throat Syrup—page 205

Preserving Herbs and Flowers

While it's always fun to work with fresh flowers and herbs, unfortunately they just don't stay in season as long as we'd like. They can, however, be dried or frozen for use throughout the rest of the year. Both forms will retain similar medicinal and healthful benefits, although dried offers a wider range of uses and is not reliant upon electricity to stay fresh.

Dried flowers and herbs can be used in all projects in this book, unless noted otherwise. Frozen flowers and herbs work best for making soaps, vinegars and other water-based projects. Because they contain moisture, they won't mix into oil-based items such as salves, lip balms or body butters.

(continued)

To dry fresh flowers and leaves, collect them on a preferably sunny mid-morning when their volatile oils are at peak level. Bring them inside and spread them out in a single layer over a clean dish towel, out of direct sunlight but in a location that gets good air circulation. Turn each piece over once or twice per day until completely dry. Depending on humidity levels and temperature in your house, this could take anywhere from two days to a full week.

Some herbs, such as thyme, rosemary, hyssop, dill, parsley, basil, lemon balm and many more, can be hung upside down in small clusters tied together with kitchen twine. Keep them out of direct sunlight and take them down as soon as they dry or they'll fade and get dusty.

For quickest results and very humid climates, you can also use a dehydrator. Remember to keep the temperatures under 110°F (43°C), in order to best preserve color, flavor and medicinal potency.

To see if a flower or herb is completely dry, rub a piece between your fingers. It should feel crisp and crumble easily. If not, just dry a bit longer. Before storing, strip leaves and flowers from stems. The stems can be composted or bundled together and saved to use as fire starters in the winter. To preserve aromatic essential oils within the plant and to extend shelf life, don't crush or powder the herbs until right before you're ready to use them in a recipe or project.

Store in clean, dry glass jars in a cool area out of direct sunlight. The shelf life for most dried herbs and flowers is six months to a year. Some, such as dandelion flowers, will fade and lose their color sooner than that. When you spot a drab herb in your collection, it's a good sign that it's past its prime.

Many flowers, such as dandelions, violets and rose petals, freeze well when spread in a single layer in heavy-duty freezer bags for around six to nine months. You can also make teas with fresh plants, then strain and freeze in ice cube trays. Once they're completely solid, pop out the cubes and store them in labeled freezer bags for up to one year.

Flowers and herbs can most often be used directly from the freezer in a recipe that requires fresh flowers. Once fully thawed, they'll be a little on the mushy side though. Teas can be thawed overnight in the refrigerator.

If you're not sure if your favorite herb or flower will freeze nicely, the best way to find out is to take a few leaves or petals, freeze them for one week, then see what the result is. In the majority of cases, the plant will freeze fine. In the worst case, you can compost the test result, but you'll still have learned something new!

Infusing Oils

By steeping herbs and flowers in oil, their beneficial properties can be harnessed for use in soaps, salves, lotions and other homemade products. Be sure the plant matter is dry before infusing. Water trapped in the oil can cause a cozy spot for bacteria and mold to grow.

There are three basic methods of infusing oil:

THE TRADITIONAL SLOW METHOD

This way requires the most patience and time, but results in a strongly infused and potent oil.

Fill a glass canning jar about one-fourth to one-half of the way with dried herbs or flowers. Next, fill the jar, almost to the top, with your chosen oil. You have a wide variety of options when it comes to oils, though some of the most commonly used ones include olive, sunflower and sweet almond.

Cap the jar and tuck it away in a cool, dark cupboard for four to six weeks, shaking occasionally. A cool, dark area is suggested since too much exposure to heat and light may begin to degrade the quality of the herbs and oils over the extended length of the infusing time.

THE WARM SUNNY-WINDOW METHOD

This process gets a jump-start from the natural heat of sunshine and still results in a high-quality oil.

Fill a glass canning jar about one-fourth to one-half of the way with dried herbs then top off with oil, just as you would for the traditional slow method. Secure a piece of cheesecloth or a coffee filter over the jar with a rubber band and place it in a warm sunny window. This breathable layer allows for any potential condensation to escape, but will keep dust and flies from contaminating the oil.

Depending on how hot it gets, your oil may be sufficiently infused for use within three to five days. If you'd like to keep infusing past this time, to obtain a stronger oil, tuck it away in a cabinet for several more weeks. Short-term exposure to sunlight and heat is okay, but in the long term may cause the quality of the herbs and oils to degrade.

THE QUICK METHOD

This method works best if you don't have the time or desire to wait days or weeks to produce an infused oil. The finished oil might not always be quite as strong as the traditional slow-infused oil, but should still have noticeable benefits. Because it's solid at cooler room temperatures, coconut oil does best when infused this way.

Fill a glass canning jar about one-fourth to one-half of the way with dried herbs or flowers. Next, fill the jar almost to the top with your chosen oil, just as you would for the traditional slow method or warm sunny-window method above, but don't cap the jar. Instead, set the uncovered jar down into a saucepan containing a few inches of water, forming a makeshift double boiler of sorts. Place the pan over a low burner and heat for around two hours. Keep an eye on things while you do this, to ensure that all of the water doesn't evaporate. If the water begins simmering or boiling, the heat is too high and should be turned down. You don't have to be precise, but try to keep the temperature somewhere around or under 115°F (46°C) so you don't accidentally cook your herbs. After two hours have passed, remove the jar from the pan and set aside to cool.

(continued)

You can also perform the quick method by infusing the herbs and oil directly in a slow cooker set to warm for two to four hours. Some slow cookers reach too high of a temperature to do this effectively, so you'll need to experiment with how your particular model works.

Once the oil has sufficiently infused via your preferred method, strain it through a fine mesh strainer or several layers of cheesecloth. Store the infused oil in a clean, dry jar in a dark, cool place, such as a cupboard. Sunlight and heat will shorten its shelf life, but when properly stored, infused oil should stay fresh around nine months to a year.

Oils and Cosmetic Butters

There are a tremendous variety of oils and cosmetic butters available via the Internet and, increasingly, local stores as well. Sometimes, it's hard to choose which ones are the best to use.

When you first venture into making your own products, it's probably easiest to just grab some basic olive, sunflower and coconut oils from your local grocery or health food store. As long as they seem to have a fairly high turnover rate and the oils appear fresh, that's perfectly fine to do.

As you fine-tune your cosmetic-making skills, however, you may want to branch out into more exotic oils. For those, you can use one of the many vendors to be found online, some of which are listed in the resource section. Although it tends to appear more costly upfront because of shipping and buying in bulk, when you work out the price per ounce or gram, the ingredients obtained online are usually a better bargain and higher quality than grocery store oils.

The shelf life estimates of the oils and butters noted here are only guidelines and will vary widely depending on the quality and age of the oil when you buy it. Store in a cool area, away from direct heat and sunlight, and they may very well last even longer than listed.

Apricot Kernel Oil—a light yet nourishing oil that softens and moisturizes, and is suitable for all skin types. Apricot oil absorbs readily and helps relieve eczema and other itchy skin conditions. Shelf life is around 12 months.

Argan Oil—absorbs quickly and is wonderful for hair and nails. It improves and repairs skin, reduces the appearance of wrinkles and can be used in formulations to prevent stretch marks. It's expensive, so if it's out of your budget, try using sweet almond or another easily absorbed oil instead. It won't have the same array of benefits, but it will still produce a nice product. Shelf life is 18 to 24 months.

Avocado Oil—a rich oil, high in B vitamins and essential fatty acids. It does well in hair care recipes and is useful for those with sensitive or irritated skin. Since it's pressed from the fruit, avocado oil is an excellent choice for those with tree nut allergies. Shelf life is around 12 months.

Babassu Oil—a great substitute for those who are allergic to coconut oil. Babassu oil is moisturizing, slightly cooling and good for dry, damaged skin and hair. Shelf life is 18 to 24 months.

(continued)

Castor Oil—a thick oil that lends a glossy shine to homemade lip balms, protects skin and has mild antifungal properties. Its low comedogenic status means it's unlikely to clog pores. In soap recipes, it helps boost lather. Shelf life is 24 to 36 months.

Cocoa Butter—rich and creamy, high in vitamin E and other antioxidants, helps soothe and protect skin. The unrefined version has a strong chocolate-like scent that carries through to the finished product. This works really well with some essential oils such as peppermint, but in other cases, you may wish to use a refined version so it doesn't overpower. Cocoa butter also adds hardness and a creamy lather to soap recipes. Shelf life is around 24 to 30 months.

Coconut Oil—melts at 76°F (24°C), moisturizes and protects skin. Coconut oil is popular for use in hair masks and treatments, and its antibacterial properties make it a good addition to homemade deodorant recipes. In soap, it contributes to a hard bar and lots of lather. Some people experience redness and dry skin after using coconut oil for an extended period of time, and it has also been known to exacerbate acne. In that case, babassu oil makes a fine substitute in virtually all applications. Coconut oil is available in unrefined or refined form. Unrefined oil is suggested for use, since it may contain beneficial properties lost in the refinement process, but refined can be used equally as well if that's what you have available. For soap making, refined oil is often the better choice due to cost. Shelf life is 18 to 24 months.

Grapeseed Oil—a light oil that absorbs quickly, without leaving a greasy feeling. It's suitable for those with oily or acne-prone skin. Grapeseed oil also works well as a massage oil or blended with heavier oils to improve absorption. Shelf life is 6 to 9 months.

Hemp Seed Oil—a rich, nutritious oil that's excellent for skin and hair care products. It's wonderful for dry, broken skin and is often used in formulations for eczema and psoriasis. The unrefined oil is a deep green color and should be kept in a very cool area or refrigerated when not in use. Sometimes, confusion exists about hemp seed oil and its connection to cannabis. The oil does not contain detectable levels of THC and is perfectly legal to use. Shelf life is around 12 months.

Jojoba Oil—a liquid plant wax that closely mirrors how our skin's sebum performs. Because of this, it's outstanding for hair, scalp and skin care. Jojoba is considered non-comedogenic, making it excellent for problem skin, while at the same time able to soften and soothe very dry skin. Jojoba oil is quite stable, with a shelf life of at least 3 to 5 years.

Kokum Butter—a hard and flaky cosmetic butter. Combine it with other oils and ingredients to help treat dry, cracked, inflamed or damaged skin. It also makes a good substitute for cocoa butter. Shelf life is 18 to 24 months.

Mango Butter—rich and creamy, moisturizes and softens skin. It can soften the appearance of wrinkles, so it is often used in antiaging products. It can usually be interchanged with shea butter in recipes. Shelf life is 18 to 24 months.

Meadowfoam Seed Oil—has a long shelf life and helps extend the shelf life of other, more fragile oils in a product in which it's included. Meadowfoam seed oil is moisturizing and softens hair and skin. It makes a good substitute for jojoba oil. Shelf life is 36 months.

Neem Oil—a strongly scented and powerful oil, used for treating skin conditions such as acne and psoriasis. It has antimicrobial, antiviral, antifungal and antiparasitic properties and repels lice, ticks, mosquitoes and other pests. Because of the strong smell, it's recommended to use neem in small amounts. If pregnant or nursing, consult with your midwife or health care provider before using neem-containing products. Shelf life is 18 to 24 months.

Olive Oil—a readily available oil that works well in most cosmetic recipes and with most skin types. In the supermarket, olive oil is available in grades ranging from dark green extra virgin to a more refined, light-colored oil. All types of olive oil will work for the recipes in this book. Be aware that many store-brand light olive oils are cut with canola oil to reduce costs and are often past their prime. They'll still work in your soap recipes, but your bars may yellow or go rancid sooner than if you purchased a higher quality product from online shops that deal specifically in soap making supplies. Shelf life is 12 months.

Rice Bran Oil—excellent for use in eye creams and serums, since it may help reduce the appearance of dark circles and under-eye puffiness. Rice bran is also a good choice for shampoo bars and hair care recipes. Shelf life is around 12 months.

Rosehip Seed Oil—a premier antiaging oil that helps smooth the appearance of wrinkles, regenerates skin and reduces scars. It's light, nongreasy, absorbs quickly and doesn't leave your skin feeling oily. Rosehip seed oil should be stored in a cool location or your refrigerator. Shelf life is around 6 to 12 months.

Sesame Seed Oil—a medium-weight oil that's high in vitamin E and may be useful for dry skin. Shelf life is 12 months.

Shea Butter—high in vitamins A and E, ideal for treating dry, weathered or damaged skin. Unrefined shea has a rather strong scent that some find unpleasant. If that's the case for you, look for a refined version that hasn't been processed with bleach or chemicals. Avoid extreme temperature fluctuations and overheating, or your shea butter may develop graininess. Shelf life is 12 to 18 months.

Sunflower Oil—a light, non-comedogenic oil that's high in lecithin and vitamins A, D and E. Sunflower is one of the best oils for applying to broken, damaged or aging skin. Shelf life is 9 to 12 months.

Sweet Almond Oil—suitable for most skin types. It's high in fatty acids, anti-inflammatory, softens skin and may help improve hair health and growth. It makes for a good massage or after-bath oil. Shelf life is around 12 months.

Tamanu Oil—a quality, unrefined tamanu oil has a distinct, deep scent. If you have tree nut allergies, consult with your physician first to determine if you should use tamanu oil. It's remarkable for treating scars, sores, stretch marks and a variety of skin conditions. Its antibacterial properties make it a good addition to acne formulations, and with its anti-inflammatory traits, it's a nice addition to sore-muscle salves and balms. Shelf life is 12 to 18 months.

Additional Ingredients

While herbal-infused oils can be useful and wonderful all on their own, they can also be turned into salves, soaps, lotions, creams and much more. In order to do that, you'll need one or more of the additional items listed below. I try to source most of my ingredients from local grocery or health food stores, but some specialty items may need to be ordered online. See the Resources section of this book (page 242) for recommended vendors.

Alkanet Root Powder—a plant-derived dye that can be used to color homemade cosmetics. Depending on how much you use, you can obtain shades ranging from pale pink to ruby red. In soap, however, the high alkalinity causes alkanet root to turn purple instead. If you're pregnant, check with your midwife or doctor before using alkanet.

Aloe Vera Gel—a clear, thick gel extracted from the leaves of aloe plants. It's great for treating skin irritations, burns and bug bites. Look for aloe vera gel near the pharmacy or sun care area of your local grocery or drug store. You can also find it in most health food stores. Even the most natural brands will have some type of preservative, but avoid synthetically colored gel or those with a lot of additives. The recipes in this book were developed and tested using a thick gel. If your brand of aloe is water-like, you'll probably need to use less of it, and the end product may turn out differently.

Annatto Seed Powder—gives soaps and cosmetics a yellow to orange tint, depending on how much you use. It tends to work best when mixed with or infused in the oil portion of your recipe.

Arrowroot Powder—a white, lightweight starch that helps absorb excess oil in some recipes. Look for arrowroot powder or starch in the gluten-free baking section of your local supermarket or health food store. If you can't find any, you can use cornstarch for a similar action in many recipes.

Baking Soda—(also known as sodium bicarbonate) a common, natural baking ingredient. It helps soften water, making it a great addition to bath salts. Combine it with citric acid to make fizzing bath salts. Along with vinegar, it's commonly used as an inexpensive and nontoxic cleaning agent for your home.

Beeswax—a faintly honey-scented yellow wax, produced by honeybees. It helps thicken creams and hold salves and lotion bars together. It has beneficial skin-softening properties and helps your skin retain moisture.

Beetroot Powder—does best dissolved in the water portion of your recipe when making lotions and creams. When added directly to lip balm, it tends to not dissolve properly and feels gritty. In soap, beetroot turns from a pretty pink to a very sad and dull shade of tan.

Candelilla Wax—a vegan alternative to beeswax, made from the leaves of a small shrub bearing the same name. You don't need as much candelilla to harden a recipe. Instead, use a little over half as much as the amount of beeswax called for. For example, if a recipe calls for 5 grams of beeswax, try 3 grams of candelilla. Be aware that candelilla wax sometimes has a strong smell that carries through to the finished product. It also tends to make a shinier end product than beeswax.

(continued)

Castile Soap—a mild and gentle all-purpose liquid soap that can be used in a variety of body, hair and cleaning recipes. You can find it in most health food stores and in many supermarkets.

Chlorella—a single-celled algae used as a nutritional supplement. For our purposes, it makes a great colorant to tint lip balm and soap a pale green.

Citric Acid—a natural crystalline powder that's derived from the fermentation of fruit sugars. Pair it with baking soda in bath salt recipes to make a fun, fizzy reaction when they meet together in the bath water. Look for citric acid near the canning jars in local grocery or feed stores. You can also order it in bulk online for a much lower cost.

Clays—come in a variety of mineral-rich natural colors, including: kaolin (white and rose), bentonite (gray), French (green), Cambrian (blue) and Brazilian (yellow, purple, red and pink). Clays draw out and absorb oils and dirt, making them great for use in face masks, body powders and deodorants. They're also excellent long-lasting colorants in soap and some cosmetics.

Emulsifying Wax NF—makes lotion-making a breeze. Emulsifying wax can be sourced from plants, animals or petroleum, so read product descriptions carefully. The "NF" part means that it's National Formulary approved, or standardized, and is the type used to develop the recipes in this book. If you use a general emulsifying wax without the "NF" label, it may not work in quite the same way. See the Resources section (page 242) in the back of this book for a recommended supplier of vegetable-sourced emulsifying wax.

Epsom Salt—often used in baths to relieve sore and achy muscles or as a scrub for exfoliation purposes. There's also evidence suggesting that some of the magnesium and sulfate in Epsom salt is beneficially absorbed via the skin while bathing. Look for Epsom salt in the pharmacy section of your local grocery store.

Essential Oils—strong concentrated extracts distilled from flowers, herbs and other plants. It takes a massive amount of plant material to produce just a tiny bit of essential oil. Because of this high cost in plant life, essential oils can be quite expensive. They're also deceptively powerful and can easily be overused. Essential oils are suggested in some recipes for fragrance or to complement a product's effect, but this book takes the position that employing the benefits of a whole plant is generally preferable to using an extract.

Honey—a wondrous product from the beehive! Its antibacterial nature makes it a strong ally when fighting wounds and other skin afflictions that just won't heal. It can be used directly, or infused with herbs, for a skin-softening face wash. Taken internally, it may help seasonal allergies, ulcers and a host of other minor ailments.

Neem Powder—derived from an evergreen tree, native to India. It's an effective pesticide and insect repellant. Pregnant women should not use neem without consulting their midwife or health care provider first.

Oats—soothe rashes and skin inflammation. Most grocery stores carry both regular rolled oats and certified gluten-free oats for those with sensitivities.

Sea Salt—can usually be found in the baking section of most grocery stores. I usually buy coarse sea salt for scrubs and bath soaks and then grind it in an electric coffee grinder if a finer product is needed.

Stearic Acid—naturally derived from vegetable or animal fats, then further processed to make white waxy flakes that can be used to help thicken lotion and cream recipes. I find it especially helpful to stabilize creams made with beeswax but no emulsifier.

Sunflower Wax—another vegan option to use instead of beeswax. It has very firm holding power, which means you only need a fraction of it to replace beeswax in a recipe. It has no detectable odor and tends to leave finished projects a bright white unless tinted with a natural colorant.

Vegetable Glycerine—a clear, sweet liquid used to soften and moisturize skin. It's also useful for making alcohol-free herbal tinctures. A small amount can be added to toners to keep them from being too drying, but if you add too much, your end result may be sticky.

Vinegar—a common astringent and acidic liquid that can be used in hair and body care, home remedies and natural cleaning recipes. For skin, hair and health applications, use a high-quality apple cider vinegar. For household use, common plain white vinegar will be fine.

Washing Soda—made from sodium carbonate and can be found in the laundry section of many grocery stores. It's used in homemade laundry detergent recipes to more thoroughly clean clothes.

Witch Hazel—an anti-inflammatory and astringent that tones and tightens skin. It's particularly well suited to treating varicose veins, hemorrhoids, bruises and rashes, such as those caused by poison ivy. Look for witch hazel in the pharmacy section of your local grocery store, near the rubbing alcohol.

Substitution Tips

You'll get the best results from the recipes in this book if you follow the ingredient list and directions carefully. Sometimes though, allergies, individual preferences or ingredient availability makes that impossible to do. At other times, you may want to put your own personal spin on a recipe and use it merely as a jumping-off point for a completely new creation you have in mind. While the following tips should help with substitutions, be aware that it may take several tries and some experimentation to get an adapted recipe to turn out right.

If a recipe calls for a type of oil that you don't have available, try substituting one with similar properties. For example, hemp seed oil is a rich, nutritious oil that's good for your skin. Avocado shares many of the same benefits and characteristics and will usually make a fine substitute for hemp. If you don't have either one available to you, though, perhaps try some

(continued)

olive oil instead. It might not always work in the exact same way, but almost any liquid oil can be substituted for another. If, for some reason, it doesn't work out, make a note of it and use your newfound knowledge to make an even better product next time!

Shea and mango butter have a similar texture and can usually be interchanged. Kokum and cocoa butters are both very hard and can often be substituted for each other. You might not always need as much of a hard butter as you would a soft butter. So, if you have a recipe that calls for 50 grams of shea butter, you may only need 40 grams, or less, of cocoa butter to replace it. Start by adding a small amount and see how it does. You can always add more of something if needed.

Since coconut oil melts readily above 76°F (24°C) and instantly as it comes in contact with warm skin, I tend to categorize it with liquid oils. If you need to substitute something for it in soap, the best option is babassu oil. In lip balms, lotions and salves, use babassu or a liquid oil, such as sunflower or olive.

Vegans and those who need to avoid beeswax can substitute candelilla or sunflower wax instead. Keep in mind, however, that these are not direct one-to-one substitutions. It only takes a little over half as much candelilla wax to firm and bind a product as it does beeswax. You need even less sunflower wax, about one-quarter as much. This is a rough formula to use as a starting guideline; individual recipes that you're converting will still need a bit of experimenting to get right:

10 GRAMS BEESWAX = 5 TO 7 GRAMS CANDELILLA WAX = 2 TO 4 GRAMS SUNFLOWER WAX

Ingredient quality, texture and other such properties tend to vary quite a bit between suppliers and even within batches of the same product. As you become more familiar with how an ingredient acts and feels in the recipes that you try, you'll build an inner awareness of when something needs adjusting, and will hopefully become more comfortable trying out bolder substitutions.

Preservatives, Antioxidants & Shelf Life

One of the great benefits of making your own natural care products is the ability to avoid synthetic ingredients and preservatives that are potentially harmful to your health. The tradeoff, of course, is that handmade products will not have the longevity that their store-bought counterparts do.

SHELF LIFE

The shelf life of the recipes in this book will vary widely, based on the freshness of the ingredients that you start with, the cleanliness of your equipment, how and where the product is stored and whether or not it contains water-based ingredients.

Items that have no water in them, such as lip balm, salves, balms, lotion bars, bath salts and bath scrubs will have a longer shelf life than lotions and creams containing water. Some oils, such as grapeseed, have a relatively short shelf life of six months. Any product containing that oil will have a shortened shelf life to match. Conversely, jojoba is very stable and can stay fresh for three to five years. Combined with just beeswax, it makes a product that could quite likely last for at least half a decade.

Generally, though, you can assume that lip balm, salves, lotion bars and so forth have an estimated shelf life of around 6 to 9 months, or possibly longer. Storing your creations in direct sunlight or high heat will cause the quality to deteriorate much more quickly.

ANTIOXIDANTS

Oil-based products won't mold or grow bacteria, but they will turn rancid. You'll know they're well past that point when they start smelling unpleasant and like old oil. While you can add antioxidants to slow down rancidity, you won't be able to completely stop it. Two popular antioxidants include vitamin E and rosemary extract.

Vitamin E is fairly easy to find in gelcaps or liquid form. While it's also terrific for skin care and minimizing scars, try adding the contents of one gel cap or around 1% to lip balms, salves and other such recipes to help lengthen shelf life.

Rosemary Extract is a CO_2 extract of rosemary, not to be confused with the essential oil. It helps to protect oils from rancidity. You only need an amount as small as 0.1% of the recipe to be effective. To best protect its potency, don't melt it with waxes and butters; wait until hot mixtures have cooled slightly before adding. Rosemary extract can also be added to bottles of more fragile oils such as hemp, rosehip and grapeseed to help them last longer in storage. Shelf life is around five years, making this ingredient a good long-term investment.

While vitamin E and rosemary extract will help slow down oxidation of oils, they won't kill germs, so are not considered preservatives.

PRESERVATIVES

Water-Based Items, such as lotions and creams, can provide the right environment for mold and bacteria to grow. When making these, use the utmost care in keeping everything meticulously clean. Sanitize your mixing utensils and jars by running them through your dishwasher if it has a sanitize cycle, or put them in boiling water for ten minutes.

Herbal Tea Infusions are more likely to shorten your lotion's or cream's lifespan, which is why I often like to use herb or flower-infused oil instead.

If you choose not to use a preservative in a handmade lotion or cream, make a small batch at a time, store it in your refrigerator and use it up within two weeks. This will work fine for personal use, but when gifting or selling a product, you'll want it to last longer than that.

Thanks to consumer demand, a handful of companies have made some exciting developments by creating preservatives that are derived from natural sources such as elderberry, aspen, fermented radishes and probiotics. While they're still being tested by individuals, and some may be milder-acting than their synthetic counterparts, it's a promising step for those who want to be as natural as possible but still offer a safe, quality product to the public.

SOME NATURE-DERIVED PRESERVATIVES TO CONSIDER

Natapres is an EcoCert-approved liquid preservative that's derived from radish root ferment filtrate, honeysuckle and aspen bark. Stir 2 to 3 grams into the lotion or cream recipes in this book, once they've cooled to under 122°F (50°C). Extra can be added, at a rate of 3% to 10%, for antiacne benefits. (For example, if all of the ingredients in your recipe add up to weigh 100 grams, you could use 3 to 10 grams of this nature-derived preservative for added antiacne benefits.)

Leucidal Liquid SF is derived from a lactobacillus ferment and is REACH compliant and salicylate free. Stir 4 grams into the lotion or cream recipes in this book, once they've cooled down to under 104°F (40°C).

Phytocide Aspen Bark is a water-soluble powder that has no- to low-irritation potential. It's GMO free, REACH compliant and can also be used as a skin-conditioning agent. Stir 2 to 3 grams (1 to 1½ tsp) into the lotion or cream recipes in this book, once they've cooled to under 140°F (60°C).

Some handmade cosmetic crafters will feel more comfortable using a stronger synthetic preservative in their creations, and that is certainly fine too. Consider the thought that a handmade lotion containing 1% of a synthetic preservative is still a more wholesome option than most store-bought products containing multiple types of synthetics and unpronounceable chemicals. The final decision on whether to use synthetic, natural or no preservatives in your creations is an individual one for each reader to make.

See the Resources section in the back of this book (page 242) for information on where to buy antioxidants and preservatives.

Equipment You'll Need

You don't need a lot of fancy, costly equipment to get started making your own natural products. Much of what's required is probably already in your kitchen or can be found locally.

Hand Mixer—The lotions, creams and body butters in this book were developed using an inexpensive hand mixer. While you should be able to use a stand mixer just as well, you may end up with differing results if you use an immersion or standard blender.

Electric Coffee Grinder or Mortar and Pestle—For some recipes, dried herbs and flowers need to be powdered or coarsely ground. An inexpensive electric coffee grinder or the more traditional mortar and pestle will do the job nicely.

Fine Mesh Strainers—These are handy for sifting powdered herbs or straining infused oils and teas. I like to keep two on hand when making things, one for dry ingredients and one for liquids.

Glass Canning Jars—Canning jars are pretty much indispensable in my mind! They're tough, designed to withstand heat and have handy measurement markings on the side. The smallest 4-ounce (125-ml) jars are perfectly sized for storing lotions, salves and such. Half-pint (250 ml) and pint (500-ml) jars can be used for infusing oils, steeping teas and storing herbs.

Digital Scale—While you can measure ingredients by volume, it's not always as reliable as measuring by weight. For the most consistent results, a digital scale is recommended. You can find a good one for a reasonable price at your local big-box store, usually in the kitchen tools area. I realize that not everyone has the ability to buy one right away, so I've included some recipes that can be measured by volume as well as weight. If you plan on making soap, however, a digital scale is a requirement because the lye and oils must be measured precisely to ensure a balanced bar of soap.

Double Boiler or a Makeshift One—A double boiler, or makeshift substitute, is important to use when heating beeswax and other oils. It utilizes more of an indirect, gentle heat that's less likely to damage your ingredients or cause a fire hazard.

If you don't own a double boiler, though, don't rush out to buy one. You can create your own instead. To do so, place the contents you want to heat or melt in a canning jar or other heatproof container. An unlined empty soup or other tin can will work too and may be helpful if you're dealing with something particularly messy or hard to clean up. Set the jar or can down into a saucepan that has 1 or 2 inches (2.5 to 5 cm) of water in it. Place the pan over the burner and heat for the recommended time or until your ingredients are sufficiently melted.

Mixing Bowl, Measuring Cups, Etc.—You'll also need a variety of mixing bowls, measuring utensils and things to stir with. While you could use the items you keep on hand for regular baking and such, it's sometimes hard to clean all of the wax residue or essential oil scents out. I like to have one glass mixing bowl, a spatula and a set of measuring cups and spoons just for my projects. That way if I use a strong essential oil when mixing up a lotion one afternoon, I don't risk my mashed potatoes smelling like it at dinner that night!

Small Food Processor—I have a mini food processor that I got as a gift over 16 years ago and in spite of constant use, it's still going strong. This handy tool is perfect for chopping fresh herbs and blending small amounts of ingredients together.

How to Make Blocks of Beeswax Easier to Use

While you can purchase convenient beeswax pastilles online, most local beeswax will come in a 1-pound (450-g) or other large-sized block form. If you've ever tried grating a block of beeswax, you know it can be quite the frustrating workout!

To make measuring it a lot easier, place the beeswax block in a large tin can or heatproof glass pitcher. A can will make cleanup a breeze since it's disposable, while the pitcher will have the convenience of a spout that will make pouring the wax much easier.

Set the can or pitcher down into a large pot that has several inches of water in the bottom. You don't want to melt beeswax over direct heat, since that's a fire hazard, which is why we do it indirectly with a makeshift double boiler.

Place the pan over a low burner and melt the beeswax. This will take a long time, possibly around an hour. Keep an eye on things and check frequently that the water doesn't evaporate.

While the beeswax is melting, spread parchment paper out over several cookie sheets. You can also use freezer paper, shiny side up. Make sure the pieces are pressed very flat or your melted dots of beeswax will puddle together.

Once melted, remove from heat and pour tiny beeswax drops over the parchment paper, then allow them to cool. They won't be perfectly sized like commercial pastilles, but they'll be much easier to use than a bulky block.

You may have to return your wax to the heat a few more times to get the entire block melted, so it's something of an exercise in patience, but you only have to do it once and you'll have enough little bits of beeswax to last a very long time!

How to Measure Beeswax by Volume

For best results, use a digital scale to weigh out the amount of beeswax needed in a recipe. If you don't have one available, however, you can still measure beeswax by volume fairly accurately, if you employ the following tips and guidelines.

Grated beeswax, small beeswax drops (from the previous section) or purchased beeswax pastilles should be tightly packed into the measuring spoon. For easy release, try spraying the spoon with a spritz of baking spray first. Press the beeswax so firmly that the small pieces stick together and mold themselves to the shape of the spoon. You should be able to remove the pressed beeswax in a single dome-shaped piece. Using this technique with a standard measuring tablespoon will yield approximately 10 grams of beeswax.

Another way to measure beeswax by volume is by melting the wax and pouring it into a standard measuring tablespoon. Beeswax measured in this manner will weigh approximately 12 grams.

Preparation Times

While some of the recipes in this book are fairly quick to make, others require some degree of preparation, time and patience. Herbs and flowers need hours, days or sometimes weeks to steep their beneficial properties into water, vinegars and oil.

It's much like baking. Sure, a boxed mix is quick and easy to throw together, but a cake that's made from scratch, with fresh, wholesome ingredients and lots of loving care, is infinitely better and well worth the extra time and effort.

This is a traditional part of hand-making products and should be embraced. Enjoy watching as each stage unfolds and your raw ingredients transform into something completely new and amazing. Whenever possible, let your children help and share in the wonder and sense of satisfaction that comes when you create something that is good and useful for you, your family and the environment!

Nontoxic Herbal Skin Care

By making your own skin care products, you avoid the sketchy chemicals and preservatives often found in their store-bought counterparts.

In this chapter, I'll help take the mystery out of creating the perfect homemade lotion or cream every time. I'll show you how to grab a rose from your garden, a handful of dandelions from your backyard or a sunflower bouquet from your local farmer's market and make something beautiful, useful and good for you and your skin.

The straightforward recipes are easy to personalize using plants that are most available in your area, and they make wonderful gifts for those you love!

Honey, Rose & Oat Face Cleanser

This soap-free cleanser features wrinkle-fighting rosehip seed oil, soothing rose petals and skin-regenerating honey, making it ideal for dry, damaged or aged skin. The ground oats act as a gentle exfoliator to slough away patches of dull flaky skin, leaving a soft, clean feeling behind as it washes away. Daily use will leave your skin feeling smooth and nourished.

YIELD: FILLS A 4-OUNCE (120-ML) JAR

2 tbsp (14 g) rolled oats

¼ cup (2 g) dried rose petals

¼ cup (60 ml) raw honey

1 tsp rosehip seed oil

Using an electric coffee grinder or mortar and pestle, coarsely grind the oats and dried rose petals. In a small bowl, combine them with the honey. Add the rosehip seed oil and stir until thoroughly mixed.

Use a clean spoon to scoop a small amount into the palm of your hand. Gently rub over your face and neck. Wash off with warm water and a washcloth. Rinse your skin well and gently pat dry.

This cleanser will stay fresh for 1 to 2 months, as long as you don't introduce water into it. Over time, the honey may settle into a separate layer. This is normal and just requires a quick stir before use. Store tightly sealed, away from heat and direct sunlight.

Variation: While rosehip seed oil is one of the antiaging stars in this cleanser, if it's out of your price range, try sweet almond, hemp or sunflower oil for their moisturizing benefits instead.

Chamomile Honey Face Wash

While it may sound a little strange and sticky at first, a daily face wash of pure raw honey, used in place of soap, is a wonderful way to balance, cleanse and repair all skin types. Adding nutrient-dense flowers and herbs to the mix makes it that much better! Chamomile was chosen for this recipe because of its anti-inflammatory and mild cortisone-like effect, making this face wash perfect for anyone with red, inflamed or irritated skin. Use once or twice daily to help calm and soothe sensitive skin.

YIELD: ¼ CUP (60 ML)

⅛ cup (5 g) fresh chamomile flowers

¼ cup (60 ml) raw honey

Place the chamomile flowers in a small glass jar. Pour the honey over the flowers and stir. Cap the jar and set aside for 1 to 2 weeks, to allow the properties of the flowers to infuse into the honey. In order to best preserve its raw benefits, don't use heat to try to speed up the process.

After sufficient time has passed, you can either strain the honey, which is a rather messy job, or just work around the flowers as you use it.

To use as a face wash, rub the infused honey over your face and neck. Allow it to sit on your skin for a minute or so if you'd like.

Take a washcloth and run it under very warm water. Place the cloth over your face for 15 to 20 seconds, to allow the heat to soften the honey. Using the washcloth, gently wipe the honey from your face, rinsing the cloth out as needed. Finish with a final splash of warm clean water on your face. Follow with your favorite moisturizer, if desired.

Store the infused honey face wash in a cool, dark area. Check before each use, but as long as the flowers remain completely covered by honey, it should stay fresh for several months.

Variation: Other flowers that work well in this recipe include roses (for toning and easing redness), calendula (for all-around soothing) and violets (beneficial for complexions that tend to be dry).

Violet Flower Cleanser

Violets and their soothing, moisturizing properties take center stage in this recipe, ideal for sensitive complexions that might otherwise be irritated by standard soap-based cleaners. Aloe buffers and protects delicate skin while witch hazel gently removes dirt and other impurities, without stripping away much needed moisture. Use once or twice per day for softer, cleaner skin.

YIELD: FILLS A 4-OUNCE (120-ML) BOTTLE

½ cup (6 g) loosely packed fresh or frozen violet flowers

½ cup (120 ml) boiling water

2 tbsp (30 ml) aloe vera gel

3 tbsp (45 ml) witch hazel

FOR THE VIOLET INFUSED WATER

Place the violet flowers in a heatproof jar or small bowl. Pour boiling water over them and let steep for around an hour. The water will turn a light shade of blue. For most of the recipes in this book, simmering water is used to make floral and herbal infusions, but in the case of violets, the color is released best with boiling water. Strain, squeezing the violets as you do, which will darken the water further. Set aside 3 tablespoons (45 ml) of violet-infused water. Any remaining violet water can be frozen in ice cube trays for future use.

FOR THE VIOLET FLOWER CLEANSER

Combine the reserved violet flower water with the aloe vera gel and witch hazel. The mixture will turn from blue to a pale purple at this point. Pour into a small glass bottle or jar. Shelf life is around 2 weeks, when stored in the refrigerator.

To use, dampen a cotton ball with a small amount and gently rub over your face. Follow with a fresh water rinse and a light moisturizer, if desired.

Variation: Pansies, violas and Johnny-jump-ups are in the same family as violets and share similar benefits. They can be used as a replacement if violets are not available in your area.

Lavender Castile Soapy Facial Cleanser

This recipe combines the cleansing power of pure vegetable castile soap with the skin-soothing properties of lavender. Because castile can be slightly drying, this recipe is best suited for those with oily or combination skin types. Lavender-infused grapeseed oil adds a nongreasy way to offset the soap, while raw honey packs a potent punch against acne and other inflammatory skin conditions. Use nightly to wash away the day's grime and buildup. Follow with a very light moisturizer, such as Grapeseed & Thyme Lotion (page 85).

YIELD: 7 TO 10 USES

1 tbsp (15 ml) liquid castile soap

1 tsp raw honey

1 tsp lavender-infused grapeseed oil (see page 16 for how to infuse oil)

1 tbsp (15 ml) water

1 to 2 drops lavender essential oil, for scent (optional)

Natural preservative (optional)

In a small bowl, stir together the soap, honey and infused oil. It's normal for the soap to turn a cloudy brown color because of the honey.

Pour in the water and gently stir, just until incorporated. Add the lavender essential oil and a natural preservative, if using, and stir one final time.

Because this product is water-based, the shelf life won't be very long. Make small batches, store in your refrigerator and use within a week or so, if you don't add a natural preservative.

To use, pour around $1/2$ to 1 teaspoon of cleanser in the palm of your hand. Use your fingers to work up a lather, adding a bit more tap water if needed. Gently smooth the cleanser over your face and neck, avoiding the eye area. Rinse thoroughly with warm water and pat dry with a clean towel.

Variation: For an even stronger effect against acne, try using thyme-infused oil in this recipe instead. You could also substitute 1 drop of tea tree oil for the lavender essential oil.

Cool Mint Body Wash

This minty body wash is a refreshing treat after a long, hot summer day. Liquid castile soap gently cleanses away dirt and grime, while mint-infused witch hazel cools aloe-softened skin. A few drops of peppermint essential oil will energize and uplift your spirits while intensifying the overall cooling sensation, but if you have extremely sensitive skin, you may want to leave it out.

YIELD: ½ CUP (125 ML)

1 tbsp (1 g) loosely packed fresh mint leaves, chopped or torn

¼ cup (60 ml) witch hazel

2½ tbsp (38 ml) aloe vera gel

2½ tbsp (38 ml) liquid castile soap

Peppermint essential oil (optional)

FOR THE MINT-INFUSED WITCH HAZEL

Place the mint leaves in a small glass jar and pour the witch hazel over them. Cap the jar, shake well and tuck away in a cabinet for at least 2 to 3 days, or up to 2 weeks. Strain and set aside 2½ tablespoons (38 ml).

FOR THE BODY WASH

In a small bowl, combine the reserved mint-infused witch hazel and aloe vera gel. Mix well until the aloe is completely dissolved into the witch hazel. Add in the castile soap and gently stir.

Pour the finished body wash into a bottle for use in the shower. While glass is nonreactive and preferred for storing most homemade products, it's safer to use plastic around tubs and showers.

To use, pour a small amount into the palm of your hand then rub both hands together to form a light lather. You can also use this with a bath puff for even more bubbles and cleansing action. Rub over your body, rinse well and enjoy the fresh clean feeling it leaves behind.

Forsythia Clear Skin Toner

The cheerful yellow flowers of the popular springtime shrub forsythia are said to possess acne-fighting and anti-inflammatory properties, making this toner a suitable treatment for skin that tends toward redness and breakouts. Witch hazel gently lifts away dirt and grime, while glycerin ensures your skin stays smooth and hydrated, without the need for additional oils. Use once or twice a day to help tame oily and acne-prone complexions.

YIELD: 4 OUNCES (120 ML)

½ cup (6 g) loosely packed fresh or frozen forsythia flowers

½ cup (120 ml) simmering hot water

¼ cup (60 ml) witch hazel

¼ tsp glycerin

Variation: Thyme is another acne-fighting powerhouse and can be used instead of forsythia flowers.

FOR THE FORSYTHIA-INFUSED WATER

Place the forsythia flowers in a heatproof mug or mixing bowl. Pour the simmering hot water over them. Steep for 10 to 20 minutes or until the water has turned a light yellow color. Strain and set aside ¼ cup (60 ml).

FOR THE FORSYTHIA TONER

Combine the reserved forsythia-infused water with the witch hazel and glycerine. Stir well and pour into a small glass bottle or jar.

To use, dampen a fresh cotton ball with the toner and swipe over your face after washing. Follow with a light moisturizer, if desired.

Shelf life is around 1 month, if kept in a fairly cool location.

Dandelion Thyme Vinegar Toner & Tonic

A tincture of dandelion is often prescribed as an internal remedy for acne. It works by improving digestion and boosting liver function. Thyme contains potent compounds that eliminate many types of bacteria, including the kind that causes acne. Together, the two herbs unite in this superpowered infusion that can be applied externally, and also taken by the spoonful to deliver a one-two punch to problem skin. A small amount of raw honey can be added for an extra antimicrobial boost and to soften skin in need a bit of oil-free moisture.

YIELD: 1 1/2 CUPS (375 ML) TONER

1/4 cup (5 g) chopped fresh dandelion leaves, stems, roots and flowers

1/4 cup (5 g) chopped fresh thyme leaves, stems and flowers

1/2 cup (125 ml) apple cider vinegar

1 to 2 tsp (5 to 10 ml) honey (optional)

1/2 to 1 cup (125 to 250 ml) water for dilution

FOR THE INFUSED VINEGAR

Place the chopped herbs in a small glass jar. Pour in the apple cider vinegar. If needed, add extra vinegar until the herbs are completely covered. Stir and cap with a plastic lid. If you only have metal lids, place a few sheets of wax paper or plastic wrap over the jar before sealing, to prevent the vinegar from corroding the metal.

Shake well and allow to infuse in a cool, dark place for around 1 to 2 weeks. Strain. The shelf life of this vinegar is at least 1 year.

To use as a tonic, try mixing 1 teaspoon of infused vinegar with an equal part of raw honey and taking once daily. If you're pregnant, nursing or have medical conditions or concerns, check with your doctor before ingesting thyme-containing remedies like this one.

FOR THE VINEGAR TONER

Combine the infused vinegar with the water. Dilute the toner with enough water to make it comfortable when you rub it over your skin. If you have very sensitive skin, use the full amount of water. You may also want to add raw honey in the winter months, to prevent excess dryness. Shake well and label clearly. Store in a glass jar out of direct heat and sunlight. It should stay fresh and usable for several months.

To use, dampen a clean cotton ball with the diluted vinegar and rub over your face after washing. Allow to air-dry, then proceed with a light moisturizer, if desired.

Tip: If fresh herbs or flowers aren't available, use half as much dried instead.

Basil & Rose Kombucha Toner

Basil is a powerful herb with impressive anti-inflammatory effects and has also been studied for its role as an antiaging ingredient in cosmetic creams. In this recipe, it combines with cooling and skin-soothing rose. Kombucha, a fermented tea drink, may seem like an unusual ingredient for a toner, but has been shown to have benefits for you skin that are similar to apple cider vinegar. Some long-term users of kombucha-based toners have also reported noticeably younger, smoother-looking skin!

YIELD: 8 OUNCES (250 ML)

¼ cup (2 g) fresh or dried rose petals

¼ cup (2 g) fresh basil, torn

8 oz (250 ml) kombucha

Place the roses and basil in a glass canning jar and then pour in the kombucha.

Cap the jar and place it in the refrigerator to infuse for around 1 week. Strain and return to the refrigerator for storage.

To use, apply the toner to a cotton ball and gently wipe over your face at night, after washing. Follow with a moisturizing cream or lotion.

Kombucha toner should be stored in a glass jar and will stay fresh for at least 1 to 2 months in your refrigerator. Discard if signs of mold appear.

Variation: Try using soothing chamomile or skin-regenerating calendula flowers instead of basil and roses.

Violet-Infused Aloe

Rub this soothing gel over mild irritations such as sunburn, bug bites, rashes, dry skin, razor burn and minor scrapes. The natural skin-calming and anti-inflammatory properties of aloe and violet, combined with its coolness from being stored in your refrigerator, will usually bring about rapid relief. Besides using straight from the jar, you can also incorporate it into creams or lotions, such as Violet & Aloe Moisturizing Cream (page 92).

YIELD: 1/2 CUP (120 ML)

1/2 cup (3 g) loosely packed fresh violet petals

1/2 cup (120 ml) bottled aloe vera gel

Place the flower petals and aloe vera gel in the bowl of a small food processor. Blend them together thoroughly. The mixture may get a little frothy in the process, but that's okay.

After blending, strain the now purple-colored aloe through a fine mesh sieve. You'll need to use your fingers to press and squeeze out most of it. The consistency of bottled aloe vera gel varies widely between brands; if yours is particularly difficult to strain, you may need to stir in a few drops of water to facilitate the process.

Store the finished violet-infused aloe in a glass jar in the refrigerator. It should stay fresh for several weeks or longer. For longer storage, freeze in ice trays and store individual cubes in freezer bags for 3 to 6 months. The frozen cubes can also be rubbed over sunburnt or irritated skin to cool and soothe away pain and inflammation.

➤ See picture on page 32.

Variation: Other flowers that work well in this recipe include chamomile, calendula and rose.

Thyme & Raw Honey Mask

This mask is ideal for irritated or blemished skin. Thyme is a classic antibacterial and antiacne herb, and raw honey heals and soothes a variety of inflamed conditions. Tamanu is a well-researched and amazing oil that's been added to the recipe for its ability to repair damaged skin, scar tissue and a variety of other skin ailments. French green clay rounds out the mix and helps draw out impurities from within the skin. This mask will leave your skin feeling clean without stripping away moisture.

YIELD: 1 APPLICATION

1 tsp dried thyme leaves

$^1/_2$ tsp French green clay

$^1/_2$ to 1 tsp raw honey

$^1/_4$ tsp tamanu oil

Using an electric coffee grinder or traditional mortar and pestle, grind the thyme leaves, then sift through a fine mesh strainer. This should yield around $^1/_2$ teaspoon thyme powder.

Stir the thyme powder and clay together in a small bowl, then stir in the honey and tamanu oil. If your skin is extremely oily, you may want to skip the oil and add more honey instead, if needed, until a thick paste is formed.

Using your fingers, generously spread the mask over your face and neck and leave on for 5 to 10 minutes. The honey makes the mask somewhat sticky, so it's okay if it doesn't go on perfectly smooth and even.

To remove, wet a washcloth in very hot, but still comfortable, water. Lay the cloth over your face and neck for around 30 seconds, then wipe the mask off. You may need to repeat this process a few times until the mask is no longer visible on your skin. Rinse off any remaining residue with clean running water.

Variation: If French green clay isn't available, try kaolin or another type of cosmetic clay instead.

Dried Flowers & Herbs Mask

Because of their ability to draw out dirt and deep-clean pores, cosmetic clays make terrific face masks. Try combining your favorite clay with ground flowers and herbs for an added boost of healing, soothing or bacteria-fighting properties. Below are a few recipes to get you started, but look at the list of flower and herb properties on pages 8 to 15 and get creative with what you have available!

To turn dry clay into a mask, you'll need to add enough liquid to it to form a paste that's easy to spread over your face. Those with dry or sensitive skin may choose to use moisturizing honey, milk or aloe, while someone with oily or acne-prone skin may use witch hazel.

Sage is a drying, antimicrobial herb, making the Sage Green Mask best suited for oily skin. Try mixing with witch hazel and apply to areas plagued with blackheads.

Inflammation-taming cornflower and soothing lavender pair up nicely in the pretty Lavender Blue Mask featuring Cambrian blue clay. This mask could be mixed with aloe for dry or combination skin or with witch hazel or water for oily complexions.

Powdered rose petals and pink kaolin clay make up the lovely Rose Pink Mask with astringent properties. Try mixing it with yogurt or milk to enjoy the benefits of their skin-softening alpha hydroxy acids.

YIELD: AROUND 2 TABLESPOONS (17 TO 20 GRAMS)

FOR THE SAGE GREEN MASK

1 tbsp (1 g) dried sage leaves

1 tbsp (16 g) French green clay

FOR THE LAVENDER BLUE MASK

1 tbsp (3 g) dried lavender flowers

1 tbsp (1 g) dried cornflower (bachelor button) petals

1 tbsp (16 g) Cambrian blue clay

FOR THE ROSE PINK MASK

1 tbsp (1 g) dried rose petals

1 tbsp (16 g) rose kaolin clay

Water, witch hazel, milk, yogurt or honey as needed to form a paste

Using a coffee grinder or mortar and pestle, grind the dried flowers and herbs to a fine powder, sifting through a fine mesh strainer if necessary. Stir the resulting powder into the clay until fully incorporated. Store in small jars or containers. Shelf life is 1 year.

To use, place a pinch in the palm of your hand. Add a few drops of your chosen liquid until a paste is formed. Apply to your face and leave for 5 to 10 minutes, then rinse well with warm running water. Use once per week or spot treat problem areas as needed.

Naturally Soothing Salves & Balms

Salves and balms are soft, spreadable preparations for your skin consisting of herbal oils and beeswax. They can be applied to help heal, soothe or improve various skin and health maladies.

In this chapter, I share a few of my favorite salve and balm recipes, such as Regenerating Rose Balm (page 59), loaded with skin-healing rosehip seed oil, and soothing Sunflower Salve (page 56), perfect for rubbing over areas that tend to get dry and rough, such as knees, elbows and heels.

Learn how to combine peppermint and pine to make a powerful salve that helps massage away headaches, or turn lavender into a sweetly scented and calming balm ideal for using right before bedtime.

Once you've tried a recipe and seen how simple yet effective salves and balms are, check out the section on building your own salve and share your new creations with friends and family!

Lavender, Coconut & Honey Balm

The raw honey in this balm is a wonderful skin-regenerating agent, making it perfect for rubbing over rough, dry areas such as elbows, knees and feet. Coconut oil helps moisturize and protect skin while lavender adds a sweet scent and calming element. This balm might be slightly sticky when you first apply it and takes a bit of time to fully absorb, so apply a thin layer before bedtime and enjoy waking up to noticeably smoother, silkier skin!

YIELD: ½ CUP (120 ML)

¼ cup (9 g) dried lavender flowers

½ cup (100 g) coconut oil

2 tbsp (20 g) tightly packed beeswax, grated or pastilles

2 tsp (10 ml) raw honey

Lavender essential oil (optional)

Infuse the lavender in the coconut oil using the Quick Method on page 17. Once it has sufficiently infused, strain the oil. You can store this infused oil for around 9 to 12 months before making the balm, if you'd like.

When you're ready to make the balm, combine the lavender-infused oil and beeswax in a heatproof container such as a canning jar. For easy cleanup, you can repurpose an empty tin can for this project. Set the jar down into a small saucepan containing a few inches of water, then place the pan over a medium-low burner until the beeswax has melted.

Remove from heat and stir in the honey for 3 to 4 minutes. Allow the balm to thicken, undisturbed, for around 5 to 10 minutes, then stir thoroughly for several more minutes. This extra amount of stirring will help prevent the honey from separating out of the balm.

If desired, add a few drops of lavender essential oil for scent, then spoon the finished balm into a glass jar. Massage into dry areas before bedtime and wake up to softer smoother skin.

Shelf life of the salve is 6 to 9 months, if stored in a cool location, out of direct sunlight.

Variation: Not a fan of lavender? Try using chamomile or calendula for their skin-soothing properties. If you're allergic to coconut, try using another oil such as sunflower, avocado or sweet almond instead.

Sunflower Salve

When drying sunflowers for seed, don't forget to save the beautiful yellow petals for projects such as this one! The sunny flowers are skin soothing and anti-inflammatory. Paired here with sunflower oil, which has been shown to be especially effective at healing broken or damaged skin, this double sunflower combo is perfect for smoothing over areas of dry, chapped skin.

YIELD: FILLS 3 (2-OUNCE [60-ML]) TINS

¼ cup (5 g) dried sunflower petals

Around ½ cup (120 ml) sunflower oil

1½ tbsp (15 g) tightly packed beeswax, grated or pastilles

Lemongrass or orange essential oil (optional)

Infuse the sunflower petals into the sunflower oil using one of the methods on page 17. Once it has sufficiently infused, strain the oil. You can store this infused oil up to 9 to 12 months before making the salve.

When you're ready to make the salve, measure or weigh the sunflower-infused oil and make sure you have ½ cup (120 ml). If needed, add a little more plain sunflower oil to reach that total. Place the infused oil and beeswax in a heatproof jar or container. Set the jar down into a small saucepan containing 1 or 2 inches (2.5 to 5 cm) of water, then place the pan over a medium-low burner until the beeswax has melted.

Remove from heat. If you'd like, add 4 to 5 drops of essential oil for scent at this time. Lemongrass and orange are two choices that match the bright and sunny nature of this salve perfectly.

Carefully pour into tins or jars. Shelf life is around 6 to 9 months, if stored in a cool location, out of direct sunlight.

Variation: Instead of sunflowers, you could also try sunny calendula, another wonderful skin-healing flower.

Regenerating Rose Balm

This soft balm harnesses the skin-calming properties of rose petals and the reparative action of rosehip seed oil. Shea butter is high in vitamins A and E and excellent for treating weathered or damaged skin, while sweet almond oil provides beneficial fatty acids and helps soften skin. At bedtime, dab this balm around your eyes, on laugh lines, your forehead and anywhere else you'd like to reduce the appearance of wrinkles, aging or scars.

YIELD: FILLS 3 (2-OUNCE [60-ML]) TINS

2 tbsp (1 g) dried rose petals, crumbled

Around ¼ cup (60 ml) sweet almond oil

¼ cup (35 g) shea butter

1½ tbsp (15 g) tightly packed beeswax, grated or pastilles

1 tbsp (15 ml) rosehip seed oil

Geranium or rose essential oil (optional)

Infuse the rose petals into the sweet almond oil using one of the methods on page 17. Once it has sufficiently infused, strain the oil. You can store the finished infused oil for several months before making the balm.

When you're ready to make the balm, combine the rose-infused oil, shea butter and beeswax in a canning jar or other heatproof container. Since rosehip seed oil is heat sensitive, we'll add that later. Set the jar down into a small saucepan filled with 1 to 2 inches (2.5 to 5 cm) of water, then place the pan over a medium-low burner until the beeswax has melted.

Remove from heat and let cool slightly. Stir in the rosehip seed oil. You can add 4 to 5 drops of geranium or rose essential oil at this time for scent or leave it unscented.

Carefully pour into 3 (2-ounce [60-ml]) tins or a small 4-ounce (120-ml) canning jar. Shelf life of the salve is 6 to 9 months, if stored in a cool location, out of direct sunlight.

Peppermint Pine Headache Salve

This salve contains mint to cool inflammation and pine for its mild pain-relieving properties. Tamanu oil is a wonderful addition to pain-relief salves, but if you don't have any, just use more infused oil instead. While the mint infused oil will have a light scent of its own, peppermint essential oil adds a deeper cooling sensation that really helps make this salve more effective. Massage the salve onto your temples, forehead, back of neck and between your shoulder blades when suffering from a headache. Close your eyes, breathe deeply and consciously allow the muscles of your face, jaw and shoulders to relax.

YIELD: 4 OUNCES (120 ML)

2 tbsp (2 g) dried mint leaves, crumbled

2 tbsp (2 g) dried pine needles, chopped

²/₃ cup (160 ml) sunflower or olive oil

1 tbsp (15 ml) tamanu oil

0.5 oz (14 g) beeswax

¹/₂ to ³/₄ tsp peppermint essential oil

Infuse the mint leaves and pine needles into the sunflower or olive oil using one of the methods on page 17. Once it has sufficiently infused, strain the oil. You can store this infused oil for up to 9 to 12 months before making the salve.

When you're ready to make the salve, combine ¹/₂ cup (120 ml) of the infused oil with the tamanu oil and beeswax in a canning jar or other heatproof container. Set the container down into a small saucepan containing 1 to 2 inches (2.5 to 5 cm) of water, then place the pan over a medium-low burner until the beeswax has melted.

Remove from heat and stir in the peppermint oil. Carefully pour the hot mixture into tins or jars.

Depending on your preference, you may want a softer or firmer salve. If so, just remelt the product and add a pinch more beeswax for a firmer consistency or a little more oil for a softer salve.

If your pain persists, is chronic or gets worse, check with your health care provider for further advice.

Shelf life of the salve is around 6 to 9 months, if stored in a cool location, out of direct sunlight.

Tip: Gather pine needles from the trees around your house and spread them out on a clean dishtowel for a day or two to dry. If you don't have pine trees in your area, try using a few drops of fir needle essential oil in your salve instead.

Dandelion Cuticle Balm

Try massaging this soft balm into the area around your nails several times a day to heal rough, dry cuticles and to strengthen nail beds. Dandelion flowers are a superb remedy for cracked, damaged skin. Tamanu oil has been widely studied for its remarkable abilities to treat tough skin conditions, but if it's not easily available, you can substitute with more dandelion-infused oil instead.

YIELD: 2 OUNCES (56 G)

1.75 oz (52 ml) dandelion-infused olive or sunflower oil (see page 17 for how to infuse oil)

0.25 oz (7 g) beeswax

1 tsp tamanu oil

Few drops of lavender or other favorite essential oil (optional)

Combine all of the ingredients in a heatproof jar or upcycled tin can. Set the jar down into a small saucepan containing 1 to 2 inches (2.5 to 5 cm) of water. Place the pan over a medium-low burner and heat until the wax is melted. Remove from heat.

If you'd like, stir in a few drops of essential oil. Lavender is a good choice because it helps heal damaged skin, but if you're not a fan of lavender, use another favorite scent instead. Pour the balm into small tins. Shelf life is around 6 to 9 months.

Massage into your cuticles and nails several times a day, or as needed.

→ See photo on page 52.

Tip: When picking dandelions, make sure they're from an area that hasn't been sprayed with chemicals. Also, save a few for the bees to enjoy, since they're an important early food source for them!

Create Your Own Salve

Now that I've shared a few of my favorites with you, I'd like to show you how to create your own customized salve.

YIELD: 4 OZ (113 G)

BASIC RECIPE

3.5 oz (103 ml) infused oil (see page 17 for how to infuse oil)

0.5 oz (14 g) beeswax (or 7 to 9 g vegan candelilla wax)

Look over the list of common herbs and flowers and their benefits at the beginning of this book (pages 8–15) and determine which one sounds good to use in your salve. You could try calendula for diaper rash, lemon balm for cold sores or plantain for a first aid salve, but don't let those few suggestions limit you.

Choose an oil that sounds like it best fits your skin type, or perhaps one that's easily available to you, such as olive or coconut. Infuse the oil with your chosen herb or flower.

Next, decide if you want to add any essential oils for scent or their therapeutic properties. If you're making this for a baby or someone who is pregnant or nursing, it's usually best to skip the essential oils. However, for the general population you could try skin-soothing lavender, germ-fighting tea tree oil or perhaps a few drops of refreshing peppermint.

Finally, combine the oil and beeswax together in a heatproof canning jar or, for easiest cleanup, an upcycled soup or other unlined tin can. Place the jar in a saucepan containing a few inches of water to form a makeshift double boiler. Heat the water over a medium-low burner until the oil and wax melt together.

Remove from heat, stir in the essential oil if you're using one and pour into a jar. A 4-ounce (120-ml) canning jar should be just the right size for this recipe. Allow the salve time to setup, then cap and store in a cool, dark area. Shelf life is around 6 to 9 months.

If you find that your salve is too soft, you can melt it back to a liquid state and add more beeswax to firm it up. Likewise, if it's too solid for your taste, add more oil instead.

That's all there is to it! From that basic framework, you can branch out and make bigger and better batches as you go along.

Exotic Body Butters & Lotion Bars

Body butters and lotion bars are super simple to whip up and make wonderful gifts for friends and family!

Lotion bars are something like a salve or waterless lotion, only in a more solid form. They're perfect for rubbing over dry hands, elbows, feet and heels. If you work outdoors or with your hands a lot, you'll find that lotion bars are one of the best treatments around for healing cracked, damaged skin.

While body butters share a similar ingredient profile with lotion bars, along with the same ability to nourish your skin, they have a light and fluffy consistency instead. They work well when applied after an evening bath or shower, and help to seal moisture in your skin all night.

Dandelion Body Butter

Apply a thin layer of this airy body butter at night for smoother skin in the morning. Body butters are rich, so remember that a little bit goes a long way! Dandelion flowers were chosen for this recipe since they're especially effective at relieving chapped, dry skin. Mango butter softens and helps skin retain moisture, but if it's not available, shea butter makes an equally lovely stand-in. Sweet almond oil is high in healthy fatty acids and absorbs into your skin nicely, but if you're allergic to tree nuts, grapeseed is another excellent choice. Two popular essential oil choices for a clean citrus scent are litsea cubeba or lemongrass, but feel free to use your own personal favorite or omit altogether.

YIELD: FILLS 3 (2-OUNCE [60-ML]) JARS

2 oz (56 g) mango butter

1 oz (30 ml) dandelion-infused sweet almond oil (see page 17 for how to infuse oil)

20 to 30 drops essential oil, for scent (optional)

1/8 to 1/4 tsp arrowroot powder (optional)

Place the mango butter in a heatproof jar or container. Set the jar down into a saucepan containing a few inches (7 cm) of water. Place the pan over a medium-low burner just until the mango butter melts. Overheating the mango butter may cause graininess, so remove it promptly once melted. Stir in the dandelion-infused oil.

Pour the melted butter and oil into a small mixing bowl and place it in the refrigerator for about 30 minutes or until it starts to firm up. Using a handheld mixer, beat for several minutes until light and fluffy, stopping to scrape the sides of the bowl several times.

Add the essential oil and arrowroot powder, then beat for another minute. Arrowroot or cornstarch are sometimes added to body butters to help cut some of the oily feel they have, but it's completely optional and okay to leave out if you don't have any or prefer not to use it.

Store the finished butter in a cool, dark area away from high heat and direct sunlight. Shelf life should be around 6 months.

Tip: If you live in a warm climate, you may want to slightly increase the mango butter or add a small amount of a harder butter, such a cocoa or kokum, so this recipe won't melt too easily between uses. During winter, or if you live in a cool climate, increase the amount of oil a bit if needed, so that the body butter isn't too stiff to apply.

Mint Cocoa Body Butter

Use a high-quality unrefined cocoa butter to create this deliciously decadent body butter that smells just like a peppermint patty! In this recipe, I use refined shea butter so that its normally strong, raw smell doesn't compete with the chocolate-scented cocoa butter and mint. If you prefer, though, unrefined shea will work just as well. Creamy cocoa and shea butters serve to protect and soothe skin while light and easily absorbed grapeseed oil helps offset the otherwise heavy richness of this recipe.

YIELD: FILLS 2 (4-OUNCE [112-ML]) JARS

1 oz (28 g) unrefined cocoa butter

1 oz (28 g) refined shea butter

2 oz (60 ml) mint-infused grapeseed oil (see page 17 for how to infuse oil)

10 to 20 drops peppermint essential oil

1/8 to 1/4 tsp arrowroot powder (optional)

Place the cocoa and shea butters in a heatproof jar or container. Set the jar down into a saucepan containing a few inches (7 cm) of water to form a makeshift double boiler. Place the pan over a medium-low burner until the butters have melted. Remove the pan from heat and add the mint-infused grapeseed oil.

Pour the melted butters and oil into a small mixing bowl and place in the refrigerator for about 45 minutes or until it starts to firm up. Using a handheld or stand mixer, beat for several minutes or until light and fluffy, stopping to scrape the sides of the bowl several times.

Add the peppermint essential oil and arrowroot powder, then beat for another minute. A little bit of arrowroot powder or cornstarch added to body butters will help cut some of the oily feel they sometimes have, but it's an optional ingredient.

Store the finished butter in a glass jar in a cool, dark area away from high heat and direct sunlight. Shelf life should be around 6 months. If the butter gets too warm, it may melt. That's perfectly fine; just chill and whip it again. If you live in a cooler climate and find the butter is too hard, you may want to use more oil in the recipe.

Calendula Whipped Coconut Oil

Calendula flowers are a wonderful addition to skin care recipes because of their regenerating and healing properties. Coconut oil is antibacterial, anti-inflammatory and helps moisturize and protect skin. This simple recipe combines those two powerful ingredients, creating a great all-over body moisturizer that's perfect for use during winter and the cooler months of the year. In hot weather and climates, it will tend to melt into a liquid, so you might want to consider making Calendula Whipped Coconut Butter on the following page instead.

YIELD: 4 OUNCES (120 ML)

¼ cup (2 g) dried calendula flowers

½ cup (100 g) coconut oil

Place the dried flowers in a heatproof canning jar or container. Set the jar on a digital scale and weigh the coconut oil into it.

Gently set the jar down into a saucepan containing 1 to 2 inches (2.5 to 5 cm) of water, then place the pan over a burner set to low. Keep the pan on the heat for around 1 to 2 hours or until the oil has taken on a yellow hue from the calendula flowers. Remove from heat and strain into a small mixing bowl.

Set the bowl in the refrigerator for 20 to 30 minutes or until it starts firming up. Remove from the refrigerator and beat the chilled oil with a handheld mixer until it's light and fluffy. This may take up to 5 minutes. Scoop the coconut oil into a jar and store in a cool area that stays under 76°F (24°C), the melting point of coconut oil.

Variation: Dandelion flowers are another good choice for this recipe and will result in a similarly effective moisturizer.

Calendula Whipped Coconut Butter

While coconut oil on its own is a fabulous moisturizer for some skin types, it tends to turn into a liquid mess in warm weather. This body butter combines the calendula-infused coconut oil from the previous recipe with skin-nourishing shea butter, to make a still light and airy, yet more shelf-stable, end product. I like to scent this with just a few drops of sweet orange essential oil, but other good options include peppermint, lavender, rose, lime and litsea cubeba.

YIELD: 8 OUNCES (240 ML)

½ cup (100 g) calendula-infused coconut oil (see previous recipe)

¼ cup (54 g) shea butter

Few drops of your favorite essential oil (optional)

Add the calendula-infused coconut oil and the shea butter to a heatproof canning jar or container. Set the jar down into a saucepan containing a few inches (7 cm) of water to form a makeshift double boiler. Place the pan over a medium-low burner and heat just until the shea butter is melted, then remove it promptly from the heat source to prevent it from overheating and becoming grainy.

Pour the hot mixture into a small mixing bowl. Cool in the refrigerator for around 30 minutes or until it starts firming up. Using a hand mixer, beat until it's light and fluffy. Add a few drops of essential oil for scent, if you'd like, then whip a few seconds longer.

Spoon into jars and store in a cool location, out of direct heat and sunlight. Shelf life of body butters is usually around 6 months.

Sunflower Lotion Bars

Lotion bars are convenient little items, perfect for rubbing over cracked, dry hands or other areas in need of softening. Tucked in a tin, they become more portable than lotions or creams, but are similarly effective at relieving chapped or sun-parched skin conditions. This lotion bar recipe contains nourishing shea butter and is boosted with skin-smoothing sunflower petals. If sunflowers aren't available, try dandelion or calendula flowers for a similar effect.

YIELD: ABOUT 10 SMALL LOTION BARS, DEPENDING ON THE SIZE OF YOUR MOLD

1 oz (28 g) shea butter

0.7 oz (20 g) beeswax

0.85 oz (24 g) sunflower-infused olive oil (see page 17 for how to infuse oil)

Place the shea butter, beeswax and infused oil in a heatproof canning jar or container. You can also use an empty, unlined tin can for easy cleanup. Set the jar or can down into a saucepan containing 1 to 2 inches (2.5 to 5 cm) of water. Place the pan over a medium-low burner until the beeswax is melted. Remove from heat, stir and pour into molds. You can use any type and size of candy or silicone mold that you'd like, as long as it's heatproof. Small one-inch (2.5-cm) candy molds will yield around 10 lotion bars while larger ones will yield less.

Once they're completely cool, unmold the lotion bars and store in a cool area, out of direct heat and sunlight. You can choose to store in individual tins or stack in a wide-mouth jar, with wax paper separating each layer.

To use, rub over your hands, elbows, knees and other dry skin areas. The heat from your body will quickly melt the lotion bar and leave a thin protective layer on your skin. For extremely dry and cracked hands in desperate need of relief, try using one lotion bar each night as you watch your favorite TV show. You should see significant improvement within a few days of consistent use.

Tip: To make these by volume, you can use 2 tbsp (30 ml) shea butter, 2 tbsp (30 ml) beeswax and 2 tbsp (30 ml) oil.

Violet Leaf Lotion Bars

Soothing and moisturizing violet leaf combines with rich and creamy mango butter in these handy little lotion bars. French green clay adds subtle color and helps to absorb the extra oiliness that lotion bars can sometimes leave behind, but if your skin is extremely dry, you may want to skip the clay. Use at least once daily on rough, dry spots in need of moisture. Lotion bars are especially effective for quickly getting winter-neglected feet into sandal-ready condition. Try rubbing one all over your feet before bedtime, paying special attention to your heels, then cover with a pair of socks. Get a good night's sleep and wake up to softer soles!

YIELD: 8 TO 10 SMALL LOTION BARS, DEPENDING ON THE SIZE OF YOUR MOLD

0.8 oz (23 g) mango butter

0.6 oz (17 g) beeswax

0.6 oz (17 g) violet leaf infused coconut oil (see page 17 for how to infuse oil)

½ tsp French green clay (optional)

Place the mango butter, beeswax, infused oil and French green clay in a heatproof jar or container. Set the jar down into a saucepan containing 1 to 2 inches (2.5 to 5 cm) of water. Place the pan over a medium-low burner until the beeswax is melted. Remove from heat, stir and pour into molds. You can use any type and size of candy or silicone mold, as long as it's heatproof. Small one-inch (2.5-cm) candy molds will yield around 8 to 10 lotion bars while larger ones will yield fewer.

Once they're set up and completely cool, unmold the lotion bars and store in a cool, dark place. To use, rub over your hands, elbows, knees and other dry skin areas. The heat from your body will quickly melt the lotion bar and leave a thin protective layer on your skin.

Variation: If you're allergic or don't want to use coconut oil, try babassu, sweet almond, sunflower, olive, jojoba, rice bran, apricot kernel, argan or avocado oil instead.

Cocoa Rose Lotion Bars

Creamy cocoa butter and rose-infused sweet almond oil make up these luscious lotion bars. Rose petals were chosen for this recipe because they're soothing and help tame inflamed skin conditions. Sweet almond oil is exceptional for its softening and conditioning properties and works well for most skin types, but if you're allergic to tree nuts, try avocado oil or sunflower oil instead. Rose kaolin clay adds an optional hint of color and helps minimize the oily feel that lotion bars sometimes have.

YIELD: 8 TO 10 SMALL LOTION BARS

0.85 oz (24 g) cocoa butter

0.5 oz (15 g) beeswax

0.8 oz (23 g) rose-infused sweet almond oil (see page 17 for how to infuse oil)

½ tsp rose kaolin clay (optional)

3 to 4 drops of geranium or rose essential oil (optional)

Place the cocoa butter, beeswax, infused oil and rose kaolin clay in a heatproof jar or container. Set the jar down into a saucepan containing 1 to 2 inches (2.5 to 5 cm) of water. Place the pan over a medium-low burner until the cocoa butter and beeswax are melted. Remove from heat. If you'd like your lotion bars to be scented, stir in a few drops of essential oil at this time. Pour into molds. You can use any type and size of candy or silicone mold that you'd like as long as it's heatproof. Small one-inch (2.5-cm) candy molds will yield around 8 to 10 lotion bars while larger ones will yield fewer.

Once they've set up and are completely firm, unmold the lotion bars and store in a cool, dark place. To use, rub over your hands, elbows, knees and other dry skin areas. The heat from your body will slightly melt the outside layer of the lotion bar and leave it behind on your skin to moisturize and protect.

Tip: Cocoa butter comes in two forms, refined and unrefined. A high-quality unrefined cocoa butter will smell so deliciously of chocolate, you'll want to take a bite of it! A few people find this scent unpleasant, though, so if you're one of those, use refined, unscented cocoa butter or similar acting kokum butter instead.

Easy, All-Natural Creams & Lotions

Many people feel uncomfortable with the long list of synthetic chemicals printed on the bottle of lotion they slather on daily, but it seems too complicated a product to try to duplicate at home. I hope this chapter helps put that thought to rest!

With the use of a basic vegetable-derived emulsifying wax, you can quickly and easily put together a lotion that's custom-made for your skin type. Because emulsifying wax allows you to incorporate more water into a recipe than beeswax does, you should find these lotions to be light, moisturizing and easily absorbed.

Since I also know that some people prefer the use and feel of beeswax, I've included a few beeswax-only recipes as well, with the caveat that they're a little fussier to make, but worth the effort once mastered. Because beeswax can't support the amount of water that emulsifying wax can, those recipes will feel richer, heavier and more cream-like.

Homemade creams and lotions lack the preservatives that their store-bought counterparts contain, so they'll spoil more easily. Keep them in your refrigerator and use them up within two weeks or add a natural preservative. See page 26 for more information on preserving and extending the shelf life of your handmade creations.

Basic Calendula Lotion

This simple lotion, featuring healing calendula flowers and skin-softening sweet almond oil, is gentle enough for everyone in the family to use. The basic recipe can also be used as a formula to help you branch out and create your own individualized variations. You can substitute calendula with your favorite herb or flower, use any type of liquid carrier oil that you like and substitute all or part of the water with witch hazel or aloe instead. Add a few drops of your favorite essential oil for scent and you will have your very own personalized lotion!

YIELD: 3½ OUNCES (100 ML)

1½ tbsp (22 ml) calendula-infused sweet almond oil (see page 17 for how to infuse oil)

3 tsp (6 g) emulsifying wax NF

5 tbsp (75 ml) distilled water

Natural preservative (optional)

Tip: This recipe is designed for use with emulsifying wax NF only. If you try to substitute beeswax or another type of wax, the lotion could potentially fail.

Add the infused oil and emulsifying wax to a heatproof jar. You can also use an empty, unlined tin can for easier cleanup. Measure out the water in a separate half-pint (250 ml) canning jar.

Place both containers down into a saucepan containing 1 to 2 inches (2.5 to 5 cm) of water, then set the pan over a medium-low burner. Keep both containers in the pan for around 10 minutes to allow the wax to melt and the water to heat up to a nearly matching temperature of around 150°F (66°C).

Pour the oil and wax mixture along with the hot water into a heatproof mixing bowl or measuring pitcher. As they're poured together, the separate mixtures will begin to emulsify upon contact and turn a milky white color.

Using a fork or small whisk, stir the lotion briskly for 30 seconds, then set it aside to cool down for around 5 minutes. To speed up the cooling process, place your mixing container into a bowl partially filled with ice cubes and water. Stir occasionally, for around 30 seconds at a time, as the lotion cools and thickens.

If you're adding a natural preservative, check the temperature to see if it's the proper time to do so. Recommended temperature will vary according to type, but preservatives are usually added when the lotion is cooling.

Pour the lotion into a pump-top or squeeze bottle while it's still slightly warm and runny, or wait until it fully sets up and spoon into a jar. Depending on how much air you whipped in while stirring, it should almost fill a 4-ounce (120-ml) jar. Your lotion may still need an occasional shake or stir throughout the first day to complete the thickening phase. Keep tops and lids off of your lotion container until it's completely cool, to prevent condensation from building up on the lid. If you didn't add a preservative, store your lotion in the refrigerator and use it within 2 weeks.

Aloe Mint After-Sun Lotion

The menthol in mint makes this lotion especially cooling, while aloe helps soothe overheated, inflamed skin tissue. Sunflower oil was chosen for this recipe since it's particularly effective at healing damaged skin. A few drops of peppermint essential oil contributes a heightened chilling effect along with a dash of mild pain relief. Apply this lotion as often as needed to help ease the discomfort of sunburn and other hot, flushed skin conditions. Don't feel that it's limited to sunburn relief though, it's perfect for helping you keep your cool every day during the summer months as well!

YIELD: 4 OUNCES (120 ML)

4 tsp (20 ml) mint-infused sunflower oil (see page 17 for how to infuse oil)

3 tsp (6 g) emulsifying wax NF

4 tbsp (60 ml) distilled water

2 tbsp (30 ml) aloe vera gel

2 to 3 drops peppermint essential oil

Natural preservative (optional)

Tip: Using aloe vera gel for part of the water portion makes for an especially nice lotion. If you're allergic to aloe, though, try using water or witch hazel in its place. Also, this recipe is designed for use with emulsifying wax NF only. If you try to substitute beeswax or another type of wax, the lotion could potentially fail.

Add the oil and wax to a heatproof jar or upcycled tin can. Measure out the water and aloe in a separate small half-pint (250 ml) canning jar.

Place both containers into a saucepan containing 1 to 2 inches (2.5 to 5 cm) of water, then set the pan over a medium-low burner. Keep both containers in the pan for around 10 minutes to allow the wax to fully melt and the water to reach a nearly matching hot temperature of around 150°F (66°C). Remove from heat.

Pour the hot water/aloe and oil/wax mixtures into a heatproof mixing bowl or measuring pitcher. As they're poured together, the separate mixtures will begin to emulsify upon contact and turn a milky white color.

Using a fork or small whisk, stir the lotion briskly for 30 seconds, then set it aside to cool down for around 5 minutes. To speed up the cooling process, place your mixing container into a bowl partially filled with ice cubes and water. Stir occasionally, for around 30 seconds at a time, as the lotion cools and thickens.

If you're adding a natural preservative, check the temperature to see if it's the proper time to do so. Recommended temperature will vary according to type, but preservatives are usually added when the lotion is cooling.

Pour the lotion into a pump-top or squeeze bottle while it's still slightly warm and runny, or wait until it fully sets up to spoon into a jar. Depending on how much air you whipped in while stirring, it should roughly fill a 4-ounce (120-ml) jar. Your lotion may still need an occasional shake or stir throughout the first day to complete the thickening phase. Keep tops and lids off of your lotion container until it's completely cool, to prevent condensation from building up on the lid. If you didn't add a preservative, store your lotion in the refrigerator and use it within 2 weeks.

Grapeseed & Thyme Lotion

This lightweight lotion is specially designed for those with oily and acne-prone skin. Grapeseed is a hypoallergenic, nongreasy oil that absorbs into your skin quickly. In this recipe, it's paired with thyme, an herb known for its ability to effectively wipe out the bacteria that cause acne. Witch hazel is an astringent that tones skin while reducing redness and inflammation. For an extra antibacterial boost, try adding a drop or two of tea tree oil. Lightly smooth this lotion over your face and neck daily, or as needed, for softer skin.

YIELD: 3½ OUNCES (100 ML)

1 tbsp (15 ml) thyme-infused grapeseed oil (see page 17 for how to infuse oil)

3 tsp (6 g) emulsifying wax NF

4 tbsp (60 ml) distilled water

1½ tbsp (22 ml) witch hazel

1 to 2 drops tea tree oil (optional)

Natural preservative (optional)

Tip: This recipe is designed for use with emulsifying wax NF only. If you try to substitute beeswax or another type of wax, the lotion could potentially fail.

Add the oil and wax to a canning jar or other heatproof container. Measure out the water and witch hazel in a separate half-pint (250 ml) canning jar.

Place both containers down into a saucepan containing 1 to 2 inches (2.5 to 5 cm) of water, then set the pan over a medium-low burner. Keep both containers in the pan for around 10 minutes to allow the wax to fully melt and the water to reach a nearly matching hot temperature of around 150°F (66°C). Remove from heat.

Pour the hot water/witch hazel and oil/wax mixtures into a heatproof mixing bowl or measuring pitcher. As they're poured together, the separate mixtures will begin to emulsify upon contact and turn a milky white color.

Using a fork or small whisk, stir the lotion briskly for 30 seconds, then set it aside to cool down for around 5 minutes. Stir in the tea tree oil, if using. To speed up the cooling process, place your mixing container into a bowl partially filled with ice cubes and water. Stir occasionally, for around 30 seconds at a time, as the lotion cools and thickens.

If you're adding a natural preservative, check the temperature to see if it's the proper time to do so. Recommended temperature will vary according to type, but preservatives are usually added when the lotion is cooling.

Pour the lotion into a pump-top or squeeze bottle while it's still slightly warm and runny, or wait until it fully sets up to spoon into a jar. Depending on how much air you whipped in while stirring, it should almost fill a 4-ounce (120-ml) jar. Your lotion may still need an occasional shake or stir throughout the first day to complete the thickening phase. Keep tops and lids off of your lotion container until it's completely cool, to prevent condensation from building up on the lid. If you didn't add a preservative, store your lotion in the refrigerator and use it within 2 weeks.

Rose Face Cream

This naturally colored face cream is a treat for mature skin! Roses are cooling and soothing, making them a wonderful ingredient in skin care products. Sweet almond oil is suitable for most skin types, high in beneficial fatty acids and helps soften and improve skin texture. Shea butter is high in vitamins A and E and is especially useful for treating weathered and damaged skin. Witch hazel tones and fights puffiness and inflammation.

YIELD: 4 OUNCES (120 ML)

¼ cup (4 g) loosely packed rose petals, fresh or dried

¼ cup (60 ml) simmering hot distilled water

1 tbsp (15 ml) sweet almond oil

1 tbsp (14 g) shea butter

1 tbsp + 1 tsp (8 g) emulsifying wax NF

Tiny pinch of alkanet root, for color (optional)

2 tbsp (30 ml) witch hazel

Few drops of rose or geranium rose essential oil (optional)

Natural preservative (optional)

Tip: This recipe is designed for use with emulsifying wax NF only. If you try to substitute beeswax or another type of wax, the cream could potentially fail.

FOR THE ROSE-INFUSED WATER

Place the rose petals in a heatproof jar or mug and pour the simmering hot water over them. Let steep for 20 minutes. Strain.

FOR THE CREAM

Combine the oil, shea butter and emulsifying wax in a small heatproof jar or container. If you'd like your cream to be tinted pale pink, add a small pinch of alkanet root to the oil. Set the jar down into a small saucepan containing 1 to 2 inches (2.5 to 5 cm) of water. Place the pan over a medium-low burner for around 10 minutes.

While that's melting, add the witch hazel to the jar of rose-infused water and set it down into the small saucepan as well. Both mixtures should end up somewhere around 150°F (66°C).

After 10 minutes of heating, remove both jars from the pan. Pour the oil mixture into a small mixing bowl along with the rose water and witch hazel mixture. It will turn a milky pink color right away as the emulsifying wax starts to react with the water.

Using a fork or small whisk, stir the cream briskly for 30 seconds, then set it aside to cool down for around 5 minutes. Stir occasionally, for around 30 seconds at a time, as the cream cools and thickens.

If you're adding a natural preservative, check the temperature to see if it's the proper time to do so. Recommended temperature will vary according to type, but preservatives are usually added when the cream is cooling.

Pour the cream into a jar. Depending on how much air you whipped in while stirring, it should roughly fill a 4-ounce (120-ml) jar. Your cream may still need an occasional stir throughout the first day to complete the final thickening phase. Keep the top off of the jar until it's completely cool, to prevent condensation from building up inside the lid, creating a cozy place for mold to potentially grow. If you didn't add a preservative, store your cream in the refrigerator and use it within 2 weeks.

Elder Flower Eye Cream

This eye cream contains luxurious oils designed to help fight the signs of aging. Argan is a premier oil that improves and repairs skin texture. If it's difficult to obtain, you can use easily absorbed sweet almond or rice bran oil instead, though they won't have the potent benefits that argan oil does. Elder flowers are an old-fashioned remedy for a beautiful, clear complexion, while modern research has shown them to possess antioxidants and anti-inflammatory properties as well. Rosehip seed oil is one of the best, most effective antiaging oils around. It helps regenerate skin tissue, reduce the appearance of scars and smooth out wrinkles. Mango butter is yet another wrinkle fighter that softens and conditions skin as well.

YIELD: 2 OUNCES (60 ML)

0.5 oz (14 g) elderflower-infused argan oil (see page 17 for how to infuse oil)

0.5 oz (14 g) mango butter

0.5 oz (14 g) beeswax, grated or pastilles

0.5 oz (14 g) rosehip seed oil

1½ tbsp (22 ml) distilled water

Natural preservative (optional)

Place the elderberry-infused argan oil, butter and beeswax in a heatproof jar or container. Since rosehip seed oil is heat sensitive, save it for later in the recipe. Set the jar down into a saucepan that has 1 to 2 inches (2.5 to 5 cm) of water in the bottom. Place the pan over a medium-low burner and heat until the wax has melted. Remove from heat and stir in the rosehip seed oil. Let cool to around 85 to 95°F (29 to 35°C).

In a small saucepan, heat the water slightly until it matches the temperature of the oil. The oil and water portions really need to be within 5 degrees Fahrenheit (about 3 degrees Celcius) of each other for the most successful emulsion.

Slowly drizzle the water into the oil mixture as you beat it with a handheld mixer. It may take around 30 to 45 seconds to accomplish this step. Beat for 5 to 10 minutes or until a thick cream develops.

If you're adding a natural preservative, check the temperature to see if it's the proper time to do so. Recommended temperature will vary according to type, but they're usually added when the cream is cooling.

Spoon the finished eye cream into a glass jar. If you didn't add a preservative, keep the cream in the refrigerator and use within 2 weeks.

Variation: If elder flowers aren't available, roses, chamomile, calendula and violets share similar complexion-improving properties.

Quick, Custom Herbal Cream

This simplified cream recipe designed for beginners comes together quickly, with no special emulsifiers, wax or equipment needed. It yields a thick, creamy moisturizer with a pleasing silky feel when rubbed between your fingers and over your skin. While you can add other water-based ingredients, such as rose water or witch hazel, a thick aloe vera gel tends to bring something special to this cream and yields the best results. Some herbs and flowers that do well in this recipe include, but aren't limited to: lavender, rose, forsythia, dandelion, calendula, chamomile, mint and violet leaves. Check the descriptions of the flowers and herbs on pages 8-15 and oils on pages 18-21 to learn about the various benefits the plants and oils provide.

YIELD: ALMOST FILLS A 2-OUNCE (60-ML) JAR

2 tbsp (30 ml) flower or herb-infused oil of your choice

1 tbsp (14 g) shea or mango butter

1 tbsp (15 ml) aloe vera gel

2 to 3 drops of essential oil (optional)

Add the flower or herb-infused oil and butter to a half-pint (250-ml) canning jar. Set the jar down into a small saucepan containing 1 to 2 inches (2.5 to 5 cm) of water and heat until the butter is melted. Remove from heat and place the mixture in the refrigerator for around 30 to 45 minutes or until it firms up to the consistency of a soft salve.

Using a fork, stir well. Add the aloe and essential oil, then stir vigorously for about 2 minutes. The mixture will start to turn opaque and creamy. Set it aside for 5 to 10 minutes to thicken, then stir thoroughly once more with the fork. You should now have a thickened cream.

Store the cream in a cool area or your refrigerator and use within a few weeks, or add a natural preservative to lengthen shelf life. If the quick cream begins to separate, simply whisk with a fork again until blended back together.

Smooth this cream over your hands, face and body, preferably after a bath or shower to seal in moisture. Because of the small amount of liquid in this cream, it's very rich, so a little bit goes a long way!

Honey & Chamomile Cream

This thick, rich face and body cream is ideal for those with damaged or weathered skin. It can also be used as an aid to relieve the discomfort of eczema and other itchy, dry skin afflictions. It contains chamomile, a wonderful herb with mild cortisone-like properties, along with sunflower oil, which has been shown to be an effective skin healer. Raw honey fights skin inflammation and repairs skin, while nourishing shea butter softens and protects from further damage. Lavender essential oil not only contributes a calming scent, but soothes and relieves hot, inflamed skin conditions. Because this cream is so rich, it does best when applied at bedtime, so it has time to sink into your skin overnight.

YIELD: 5 OUNCES (150 ML)

2 oz (60 ml) chamomile-infused sunflower oil (see page 17 for how to infuse oil)

1 oz (28 g) shea butter

0.5 oz (14 g) beeswax, grated or pastilles

1.75 oz (50 ml) warm distilled water

1 tsp raw honey

2 to 3 drops lavender essential oil (optional)

Natural preservative (optional)

Place the chamomile-infused oil, butter and beeswax in a heatproof jar or container. Set the jar down into a saucepan containing a few inches (7 cm) of water. Place the pan over a medium-low burner until the wax and butter are melted.

Remove from heat, pour into a small mixing bowl and let cool to around 85 to 95°F (29 to 35°C).

While the oil mixture is cooling, stir the warm water and honey together in a small bowl or cup until the honey is fully dissolved. Set aside.

Once the oil mixture has sufficiently cooled, it will be thicker and almost salve-like. Check the temperature of the water and heat if necessary by setting it down in the pan of water used to melt the beeswax and oils. When making creams with beeswax and no emulsifier, it's important that both the oil and water portions are in the same temperature range of 85 to 95°F (29 to 35°C) and less than 5 degrees apart for the most successful emulsion.

Using a hand mixer, start beating the oil mixture. Continue beating, adding a small amount of water at a time and incorporating it before adding more. It will take around 1 minute to work all the water in. Continue beating another 3 to 5 minutes, stopping to scrape down the sides of the bowl once or twice. If you decide to add lavender essential oil, do so at this time.

If you're adding a natural preservative, check the temperature to see if it's the proper time to do so. Recommended temperature will vary according to type of preservative used, but they're usually added when the cream is cooling.

Spoon the finished cream into a glass jar. If you didn't add a preservative, keep the cream in the refrigerator and use within 2 weeks.

Violet & Aloe Moisturizing Cream

This recipe incorporates the Violet-Infused Aloe from page 47. While infused aloe alone is a soothing treat for inflamed skin, it works equally well for daily skin protection when incorporated in moisturizing creams such as this one. Stearic acid (a natural fatty acid sourced from plants or animals) is a popular ingredient used to help thicken creams and lotions. If you leave it out, the recipe will yield unreliable results. Sweet almond oil is high in nourishing fatty acids and helps soften and smooth skin, while shea butter protects against damaging elements.

YIELD: 3 OUNCES (90 ML)

3 tbsp (45 ml) sweet almond oil

1½ tbsp (21 g) shea butter

1 tbsp (10 g) tightly packed beeswax, grated or pastilles

½ tbsp (3 g) stearic acid

¼ cup (60 ml) violet-infused aloe (or plain aloe vera gel)

Few drops of essential oil, for scent (optional)

Natural preservative (optional)

Combine the sweet almond oil, butter, beeswax and stearic acid in a heatproof jar or container. Set the jar down into a saucepan that has 1 to 2 inches (2.5 to 5 cm) of water in it. Place the pan over a medium-low burner until the wax and stearic acid are melted.

Remove from heat and pour into a small mixing bowl. Let cool to room temperature, then add the infused aloe vera gel and essential oil, if using. One of my favorite scent combinations for this cream is a few drops each of lavender and litsea cubeba essential oils, but you can use any scent that you prefer. Using a handheld mixer, beat for around 5 minutes or until thick and creamy.

Spoon the finished cream into a glass jar. Store the cream in a cool area and use within 2 weeks, or add a natural preservative to lengthen shelf life.

Variation: Sweet almond oil is a great all-purpose oil suitable for most skin types, but if you're allergic to tree nuts, try using sunflower or avocado oil instead. Mango butter can be used if shea is not available or tolerated.

Garden-Fresh Bath Soaks & Salts

Soak away the stresses of life with these herbal bath recipes designed to renew, revitalize or relax your mind, body and spirit.

For those times that you're feeling run-down and in need of a quick pick-me-up, try Energizing Rosemary Mint Bath Tea (page 104) or Garden Herbs Bath Soak (page 97).

Are you longing for a good night's sleep? You'll surely want to spend time relaxing in a Calming Bath Soak (page 98) or Lavender Sleepy Time Bath Tea (page 104). For an even greater sleep-inducing effect, try pairing one of these soothing bath treats with a spoonful of Chamomile Calming Syrup (page 209).

If you're a fan of that perennial fall favorite, pumpkin spice, you'll definitely want to check out Calendula Spice Fizzing Bath Salts (page 101). Just as their name implies, these easy-to-make bath salts add a fun fizz factor to tub time, much like a bath bomb, minus the hefty price tag!

Garden Herbs Bath Soak

This refreshing bath soak incorporates a variety of green herbs and leaves from the garden. Mix and match as you please, but choose several strong aromatics, such as mint, lavender leaves, rosemary, sage, thyme or pine needles for their energizing scents and beneficial circulation-boosting properties. If available, add a few leaves of violet or plantain to round out the mix and for their extra skin-soothing effect. Baking soda softens the water while Epsom salt helps ease sore muscle aches and pains. These bath salts are further scented with invigorating eucalyptus and peppermint essential oils to revitalize and uplift a tired spirit and body. As a bonus, these two essential oils are amazing at clearing sinuses, making this a great soak for when you have a stuffy nose or cold.

YIELD: ½ CUP (130 G) OR ENOUGH FOR 1 BATH

½ cup (about 12 g) chopped fresh green herbs and leaves, loosely packed

½ cup (112 g) Epsom salt

1 tbsp (9 g) baking soda

Few drops each of eucalyptus and peppermint essential oils

Reusable tea bag or a 12 x 12-inch (30 x 30-cm) square of plain muslin cloth, plus string for tying (optional)

Using a small food processor, coarsely blend the fresh leaves and Epsom salts together. Spread the salt and herb mixture out on a sheet of wax paper and allow to air dry for 1 to 2 days. The salt works to quickly pull moisture from the leaves and needles, preserving the bright green color of fresh herbs.

In a small mixing bowl, combine the dried herb salts and baking soda. Stir in a few drops each of eucalyptus and peppermint essential oils.

Pour into a small jar or, to make after-bath cleanup easier, tie the bath salts up in a reusable tea bag or a 12 x 12-inch (30 x 30-cm) square of plain muslin cloth.

To use, pour the loose bath salts into warm bathwater, or drop the bag of salts in while the water is running, and enjoy a rejuvenating bath. Because eucalyptus and peppermint essential oil are not recommended for use in young children, this bath is more suitable for older teens and nonpregnant adults.

Calming Bath Soak

This recipe combines two classic calming herbs, chamomile and lavender, in a soak designed to relax and soothe both body and mind. Oatmeal is fantastic at relieving all sorts of rashes and skin irritations while Epsom salt provides magnesium that's so important for maintaining a healthy nervous system. A few drops of lavender essential oil will add an extra element of calm to your bath, but it can be omitted if you're sensitive to the stronger scent.

YIELD: 1 CUP (240 G) OR ENOUGH FOR 4 BATHS

1 tbsp (1 g) dried chamomile flowers

1 tbsp (1 g) dried lavender flowers

1 tbsp (6 g) old-fashioned rolled oats

1 cup (232 g) Epsom salt

Few drops lavender essential oil (optional)

Combine the dried flowers and oatmeal. Using an electric coffee grinder or mortar and pestle, grind the herbs to a fine powder.

Blend the resulting scented herbal powder into the Epsom salt, then stir in the essential oil until completely incorporated. Store in a tightly sealed jar.

Add ¼ cup (60 g) of the mixture to your tub as it fills with warm bathwater. For easier cleanup, place the bath soak in a reusable tea bag or tie up in a clean sock before use.

Calendula Spice Fizzing Bath Salts

These deliciously scented fizzing bath salts carry the subtle aroma of pumpkin spice and are perfect for adding to your tub on a cool evening in late fall or winter. Calendula flowers soothe and soften skin chafed by blustery weather, Epsom salt helps ease muscle aches, while the ginger and cinnamon gently increase circulation to warm cold fingers and toes. The fun fizzing reaction comes about when an alkaline ingredient (baking soda) comes in contact with an acidic substance (citric acid). Those with delicate skin types may find citric acid a little too intense for anything other than occasional use. If that's the case, it can be omitted. The bath salts will still work and smell wonderful, they just won't be fizzy.

YIELD: ENOUGH FOR 6 BATHS

1 cup (224 g) Epsom salt

¼ cup (56 g) baking soda

2 tbsp (24 g) citric acid

¼ tsp ground ginger

¼ tsp ground cinnamon

¼ cup (2 g) dried calendula flowers

In a small mixing bowl, combine the Epsom salt, baking soda, citric acid, ginger and cinnamon.

Using an electric coffee grinder or mortar and pestle, grind the dried calendula flowers until they're powdered very finely, sifting through a fine mesh strainer if needed. Add the calendula powder to the other ingredients.

Pour the bath salts into a jar and seal tightly. Label and store in a cool area, out of direct sunlight and heat.

For a warm, stimulating bath, pour around ¼ cup (60 g) into your bath water. The salts will fizz and bubble and give off a subtle pumpkin spice scent.

Be sure to avoid getting moisture in the jar and close it tightly after each use. It's imperative that fizzing bath salts stay completely dry or they will begin to clump together in the jar. If you live in an area with high humidity, you may want to leave out the citric acid and have a non-fizzing, but still lovely, bath salt. If you plan on making these for gifts, don't make them too far ahead of time since they may lose their active properties over a long period of storage.

Note that ginger and cinnamon in your bathwater will increase circulation and may promote sweating, so if you have blood pressure problems, keep the amounts low or check with a doctor before use.

Fizzy Rose Lemonade Soak

Sweet roses and zesty lemon peel combine in these fun and fizzy summery bath salts! Roses have a cooling and astringent effect on the body, making them a great addition to hot-weather recipes. Lemon peel adds a subtle, bright citrus scent while sea salt softens and rejuvenates the skin. Pink Himalyan salt lends a pretty rosy color to this soak along with an impressive 84 minerals and superior detoxification properties, but if it's not available or affordable for you, more sea salt can be used instead. Citric acid and baking soda combine in the bathwater to make this soak a fizzy one. If you have sensitive skin or can't find a source for it, you can omit the citric acid for a non-fizzy but still amazing bath experience.

YIELD: ENOUGH FOR 4 BATHS

¼ cup (2 g) dried rose petals

1 tbsp (1 g) dried lemon peel

½ cup (145 g) coarse sea salt

¼ cup (60 g) coarse pink Himalayan salt

¼ cup (56 g) baking soda

2 tbsp (24 g) citric acid

Using an electric coffee grinder or mortar and pestle, grind the rose petals and lemon peel together, along with 2 tablespoons (35 g) of the sea salt, until they're finely powdered.

Stir the ground mixture together with the remaining ingredients, until completely distributed throughout. Seal tightly in a completely dry container.

To use, pour around ¼ cup (60 g) into your warm bathwater. The salts will fizz and bubble and give off a fun scent of pink lemonade and summer.

Be sure to avoid getting moisture in the jar and close it tightly after each use. It's imperative that fizzing bath salts stay completely dry or they will begin to clump together in the jar. If you live in an area with high humidity, you may want to leave out the citric acid and have a non-fizzing, but still lovely, bath salt.

➥   See photo on page 94.

Sore Muscle Bath Bags

Relax and ease your aches and pains with a warm bath and these aromatic salt bags. Pine, juniper and mint were chosen for their pain-relieving abilities and to complement the muscle-relaxing properties of Epsom salt and lavender essential oil. As an added bonus, the eucalyptus oil in these bath bags can also help clear stuffy noses when a cold or sinus congestion strikes!

YIELD: 3 TO 4 BATH BAGS

¾ cup (168 g) Epsom salt

4 tbsp (2 g) dried mint leaves, crumbled

¼ cup (5 g) dried pine needles, finely chopped

5 to 10 drops eucalyptus essential oil

10 to 15 drops lavender essential oil

3 to 4 reusable muslin tea bags

9 to 12 dried juniper berries (optional)

Combine the Epsom salt with the mint, pine needles and essential oils in a pint (500-ml) canning jar. Cap and shake thoroughly, until all ingredients are completely and evenly mixed together.

Divide the sore muscle salts between 3 or 4 reusable tea bags. If you don't have any on hand, you can tie the salts up in clean socks instead. Add 2 to 3 juniper berries per bag, if using, and tie closed.

Store the bags in a tightly sealed jar, to keep the aroma and essential oils from escaping.

To use, add one bath bag to the water as the tub fills, and enjoy a soothing, relaxing bath.

Tip: Gather pine needles from trees around your house and spread them out on a clean dishtowel for a day or two or until completely dry. Because they don't have high water content to begin with, they dry quite quickly. If you don't have pine trees in your area, try using a few drops of fir needle essential oil in this recipe instead.

Garden Bath Teas

Bath teas may be among the simplest of projects to make, and they're wonderfully effective and therapeutic. Essentially, you can blend almost any combination of dried herbs, flowers and spices together to make a complementary mix. Below are a few of my favorites, but feel free to mix and match the plants you have on hand to create your own personalized recipes.

The Warming Ginger & Lemon Balm Bath Tea helps increase circulation and makes the perfect bath for when you feel run down or as if you're catching a cold. If larger pieces of dried grated ginger aren't available, use half as much ground ginger instead.

The Lavender Sleepy Time Bath Tea combines relaxing lavender with calming chamomile and emotion-balancing rose. Take a warm bath in this tea, put on your most comfy pajamas and then settle in for a good night's sleep.

The Energizing Rosemary Mint Bath Tea is perfect for those times that you need a quick pick-me-up. Rosemary increases circulation and boosts your level of alertness while mint helps awaken the mind and spirit. Juniper berries add an extra burst of energetic scent, but can be omitted if they're not easily available.

YIELD: 1 TO 2 BATH TEAS PER RECIPE

WARMING GINGER & LEMON BALM BATH TEA

2 tbsp (1 g) dried lemon balm leaves

1 tbsp (6 g) dried ginger root pieces

1 tbsp (8 g) dried lemon peel

1 to 2 reusable tea bags

1 cup (250 ml) boiling water

LAVENDER SLEEPY TIME BATH TEA

2 tbsp (2 g) dried lavender buds

1 tbsp (1 g) dried chamomile flowers

1 tbsp (1 g) dried rose petals

1 to 2 reusable tea bags

1 cup (250 ml) boiling water

ENERGIZING ROSEMARY MINT BATH TEA

1 tbsp (1 g) dried rosemary

1 tbsp (1 g) dried mint leaves

1/2 tbsp (2 g) dried juniper berries (optional)

1 reusable tea bag

1 cup (250 ml) boiling water

Crumble the herbs and flowers and place them in reusable muslin tea bags. You don't need to grind larger pieces of dried herbs such as lemon peel, ginger root or juniper berries. If you don't have muslin tea bags handy, try tying the herbs up in squares of old, white T-shirts or in clean socks.

Place the tea bag(s) in a mug or other heatproof container and pour the boiling water over. Let steep for 20 minutes, then begin running your bath. Pour the tea into the tub along with the tea bag. Making an infusion first in this manner helps the bath to be stronger and therefore more effective. If you're crunched on time, though, you can just add the tea bag directly to your tub as the warm bathwater runs in. Soak your body in the theraputic water.

Beautiful
Bath Melts & Scrubs

Turn your bath into a mini-spa with these luxurious treats that leave your skin smooth, polished and moisturized.

Bath melts are little shapes of solid butters, such as cocoa and shea, blended with herbs, flowers and other things that are lovely for your skin. To use, drop one in the tub at the start of your bath. The warmth from the water will soften the creamy butter, melting it into the water and onto your skin, leaving behind a protective layer that helps seal moisture into your skin. There's usually no need to apply a body lotion after using a bath melt—they have a convenient and effective moisturizing system built right in!

Scrubs come in many forms and are used to exfoliate away dull, flaky skin. Since they're a rather intense skin treatment, it's best to only use body scrubs once every week or two. For tougher areas, such as your feet, you can use them more frequently until the level of smoothness you desire is reached. After that, move to a weekly or bimonthly maintenance schedule. You'll find several fun body scrubs in this chapter plus a couple of handy scrub shapes designed specifically for smoothing rough heels and getting your feet in tip-top shape for sandal season!

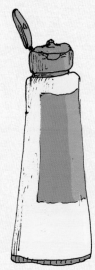

Lavender Oatmeal Bath Melts

Skin-soothing oats and inflammation-fighting lavender flowers team up in this bath melt to provide relief to itchy, irritated skin. The light floral scent relaxes and calms the mind, while the cocoa butter and sweet almond oil melt into your water-warmed skin to lock in much-needed moisture.

YIELD: 10 TO 12 SMALL BATH MELTS

5 tbsp (70 g) cocoa butter

1½ tbsp (22 ml) sweet almond oil

1 tbsp (3 g) dried lavender buds

1 tbsp (7 g) oats

Combine the cocoa butter and sweet almond oil in a heatproof jar or container. Set the jar down into a saucepan containing a few inches (7 cm) of water. Place the pan over a medium-low burner until the cocoa butter melts.

Meanwhile, grind the lavender buds and oats to a very fine powder using an electric coffee grinder or mortar and pestle. Sift large pieces out with a fine mesh sieve, to make after-bath cleanup time much easier.

Combine the melted cocoa butter and sweet almond oil mixture with the powdered lavender and oats. Pour into silicone molds and place in the freezer until solid.

Remove the melts from the mold and store in a cool, dry place. If your house stays really warm, you may want to store bath melts in your refrigerator or freezer.

To use, drop 1 melt into the tub while running warm bathwater. It will slowly melt in the water, leaving a fine layer of oil behind to seal in the moisture from your bath. Be careful as you exit the tub, since the oil may make it slippery. To make after-bath cleanup easier, you may want to tie the bath melt up in a clean sock or reusable tea bag before using, so that it catches any stray specks of herbs or oatmeal instead of leaving them on the surface of your tub.

Vanilla Rose Bath Melts

Pure shea butter and the heady scent of rose are featured in these luxurious melts that turn bath time into a replenishing treat for mind, body and soul.

YIELD: 12 TO 16 SMALL BATH MELTS

½ cup (110 g) shea butter

2 tbsp (1 g) dried rose petals

2 inch (5 cm) section of vanilla bean, chopped

Rose essential oil (optional)

Place the shea butter in a heatproof jar or container and set it down into a small saucepan containing a few inches (7 cm) of water. Set the pan over a medium-low burner until the shea butter melts. Overheated shea butter can become grainy, so be sure to remove it promptly from the heat source as soon as it is melted.

While the shea butter is melting, grind the rose petals and chopped vanilla bean together with an electric coffee grinder or mortar and pestle, to a fine powder.

Stir the vanilla rose powder and a few drops of rose essential oil, if using, into the melted shea butter and pour into small silicone molds. Place the mold in the refrigerator or freezer until firm, then remove from the mold. It's normal for the powder to settle to the bottom of the mold (which turns out to be the top of the bath melt once it's removed from the mold).

Store bath melts in a cool dry place or in a sealed container in your refrigerator or freezer. To use, drop in one bath melt as you run warm water into the tub. After your bath, as you emerge from the water, the shea butter will cling in an even layer over your skin, helping to seal in moisture. Be careful as you exit the tub, since the oil may make it slippery. To make after-bath cleanup easier, you may want to tie the bath melt up in a clean sock or reusable tea bag before using, so that it catches any stray specks of rose petals or vanilla bean instead of leaving them on the surface of your tub.

Lemon Chamomile Bath Melts

Anti-inflammatory chamomile combines with zesty lemon in these sunny melts that brighten and uplift your outlook as they soothe and seal in moisture. Lemongrass essential oil is a great choice for this recipe, adding a cheerful citrus scent for a clean and rejuvenating bath experience. Cocoa butter adds a delightful creaminess to these melts, but the unrefined version may also lend an overpowering and unwanted chocolate-like scent. If you really want the lemon fragrance to shine through, try using refined cocoa butter or substitute with barely scented kokum butter.

YIELD: 12 TO 14 BATH MELTS

2 ½ tbsp (35 g) cocoa butter

5 tbsp (70 g) shea butter

1 tbsp (1 g) dried chamomile flowers

1 tsp dried lemon peel or zest

Lemongrass essential oil (optional)

Add the cocoa and shea butter to a heatproof jar or container and set it down into a small saucepan containing a few inches (7 cm) of water. Set the pan over a medium-low burner until the butters are completely melted, then remove from heat. Overheated shea butter can become grainy, so be sure to remove the pan promptly from the heat source as soon as the butters are melted.

While the butters are heating, use an electric coffee grinder or mortar and pestle to grind the chamomile flowers and lemon zest together until finely powdered.

Stir the chamomile-lemon powder into the melted butters. For a bright lemon scent, add a few drops of lemongrass essential oil if you'd like. Pour into small silicone molds and place in the refrigerator or freezer until firm. Unmold and store in a cool area or in a sealed container in your refrigerator or freezer.

To use, drop 1 bath melt in as you run warm water in your bath. The heat from the bath will melt the butters, leaving a fine layer on your skin after bathing, sealing in moisture. Be careful as you exit the tub, since melts can sometimes make the floor slippery. To make after-bath cleanup easier, you may want to tie the bath melt up in a clean sock or reusable tea bag before using, so that it catches any stray specks of powdered chamomile or lemon peel instead of leaving them on the surface of your tub.

Calendula Spice & Honey Cleansing Scrub

This scrub polishes skin as it cleanses, leaving behind a light silky feel. Ginger and cinnamon increase circulation and warm the body as they add a delicious scent along with the vanilla extract. Calendula was chosen for this recipe since it offers multiple beneficial properties that are helpful for repairing and maintaining skin health. Sweet almond is a nourishing oil that's suitable for most skin types, but if you're allergic to tree nuts, try using olive or sunflower in this recipe instead. Mild liquid castile soap gently lifts away dirt while honey rejuvenates damaged skin. Use this delightful scrub once every week or two for smoother, silkier skin!

YIELD: 4 OUNCES (120 ML)

¼ cup (71 g) coarse sea salt

½ tbsp (7 ml) calendula-infused sweet almond oil (see page 17 for how to infuse oil)

1 tsp raw honey

1½ tbsp (22 ml) liquid castile soap

⅛ tsp ginger

¹⁄₁₆ tsp cinnamon

¼ tsp pure vanilla extract

Place all of the ingredients in a small mixing bowl and stir together until completely combined. Some brands of castile soap have a stronger scent than others, so smell the mixture to determine if it needs more vanilla or spices, and add extra of those ingredients if desired.

Spoon the mixture into a 4-ounce (120-ml) jar.

For best results, apply the scrub to skin dampened by a shower or bath. Scoop out a small amount and rub over dry spots and other places on your body in need of cleansing and exfoliation. You can also use this scrub as a hand wash. Rinse well with warm running water. Be careful if using in the shower or tub, since the oil might make the floor a little slippery.

➤ See photo on page 106.

Peony & Orange Sugar Scrub

Fresh peony petals are used to naturally color this invigorating hand and body scrub. For best color results, use dark pink or red flowers. The granulated sugar in this scrub polishes away dull flakiness and increases blood flow to the surface of the skin. Sunflower oil is added for its ability to protect and repair damaged skin. After using this scrub your skin will glow and feel silky and smooth!

YIELD: 4.5 OUNCES (130 G)

Small handful of fresh peony petals (about 5 g)

½ cup (100 g) granulated sugar

2 to 3 tbsp (30 to 45 ml) sunflower or other light oil

3 drops sweet orange essential oil

FOR THE PEONY SUGAR

Place the peony petals and sugar in the bowl of a small food processor. Blend until an even texture and color is achieved. Spread the now-colored sugar in a single layer over a sheet of wax paper and allow it to air dry for 1 to 2 days. Run through the food processor again, if needed, to break up any large chunks before proceeding with the recipe.

FOR THE SCRUB

Place the dried peony sugar in a small mixing bowl. Add the oil, 1 tablespoon (15 ml) at a time, stirring well after each addition. Continue adding oil until you've reached a consistency that you like. Add 3 drops of orange essential oil for scent. Stir well.

Store in a tightly sealed container, out of direct heat and sunlight. Your scrub should stay fresh for several months as long as you keep water out of it.

For best results, apply the scrub to skin dampened by a shower or bath. Scoop out a small amount and rub over dry spots and other places on your body in need of exfoliation. You can also use it as a hand scrub after washing your hands. Rinse well with warm running water. Be careful if using in the shower or tub, since the oil might make the floor a little slippery.

Variation: If you don't have peonies growing near you, try pink or red rose or dianthus petals instead.

Whipped Spearmint Scrub Butter

Spearmint adds an uplifting and invigorating aroma to this scrub, which moisturizes as it exfoliates. Grapeseed was chosen for this recipe because it's quickly absorbed and won't leave an excessively oily feeling behind. If that's not available, try sweet almond or sunflower oil instead. While this scrub can be used all over your body, it's especially nice for relieving and rejuvenating tired, achy legs and feet.

YIELD: 5.5 OUNCES (156 G)

½ cup (112 g) shea, mango or avocado butter

2 tbsp (30 ml) mint-infused grapeseed oil (see page 17 for how to infuse oil)

40 to 50 drops spearmint essential oil (optional)

¼ cup (50 g) granulated sugar

Place the shea, mango or avocado butter in a medium mixing bowl. For this recipe, you don't need to melt the butter first. If the brand or type of butter that you have is excessively hard, try buying from another source. You want a slightly soft texture for this project.

Using a handheld or stand mixer, beat the butter for 2 to 3 minutes or until light and fluffy. If using an inexpensive handheld mixer, you may need to periodically stop beating while making this recipe so you won't overheat the motor. Add the mint-infused oil and spearmint essential oil, then beat for an additional 2 to 3 minutes. The butter should now be light and fluffy, much like buttercream frosting.

Lightly fold the sugar into the whipped butter until it's evenly distributed. Spoon into jars for storage.

For best results, apply the scrub to skin dampened by a shower or bath. Scoop out a small amount and rub over dry spots and other places on your body in need of exfoliation. Avoid using on the face or other sensitive areas. Rinse well with warm running water. Be careful when using in the shower or bath, since the oils from the scrub tend to make the floor a little slippery.

Store the scrub butter in a cool, dry area. Shelf life should be 3 to 6 months, but will be shortened considerably if water gets into the mix.

Variation: For a relaxing scrub butter, try substituting spearmint with lavender instead.

Floral Salt Foot Scrub Bars

By blending salt and fresh flowers together, then binding them with skin-softening coconut oil, you can create a rainbow of these naturally colored scrub bars that polish and smooth rough, dry feet. Some flowers that work well in this recipe include: violets, roses, dandelions, peonies, dianthus and forsythia. For a pretty green tint, try mint or lemon balm. While most scrubs should be used only once every week or two, if your feet are particularly rough or dry, you can use more often until the level of smoothness you desire is reached.

YIELD: 4 OR 5 SCRUB BARS

¼ cup (70 g) coarse sea salt

¼ cup (5 g) loosely packed fresh flower petals

2 tbsp (27 g) coconut oil

TO MAKE THE FLORAL SALTS

Using a small coffee grinder, blend the sea salt and flower petals together. Spread the now-colored salt onto a sheet of wax paper and allow to air-dry overnight. The salt helps to rapidly dry the fresh petals, without the fading of color that normally occurs when you dry flowers. The result is brightly colored salts that last for months and look beautiful in scrub and bath salt recipes.

TO MAKE THE SALT SCRUB BARS

Melt the coconut oil in a small saucepan. Stir in the floral-colored salt. Scoop the mixture into shaped silicone molds and place in the freezer for half an hour, or until solid.

These melt easily in warm weather, so store in an airtight container in your refrigerator or freezer.

Use one or two bars during bath time to scrub the bottom of your feet. The salts will dissolve into the bathwater after their exfoliating job is done, while the coconut oil stays behind to seal in moisture, leaving your skin soft and smooth. Be careful as you exit the tub, since the coconut oil can make the floor slippery.

Chamomile Brown Sugar Scrub Cubes

These scrub cubes feature brown sugar, which acts as a gentle exfoliant to polish away dull, flaky skin. Chamomile was selected for this recipe because it helps calm and soothe most skin types. Coconut oil is an excellent antimicrobial and moisturizer, but if you happen to be allergic to it, you can replace it with another oil, such as sunflower, olive or sweet almond. Honey always makes a great addition to skin care recipes because it leaves your skin feeling wonderfully rejuvenated after it's washed off. Creamy cocoa butter binds all of these ingredients together in a convenient and easy-to-use cube form that will leave your skin feeling smooth and silky.

YIELD: 5 SCRUB CUBES

2 tbsp (28 g) cocoa butter

1½ tbsp (15 g) chamomile-infused coconut oil (see page 17 for how to infuse oil)

½ tbsp (7 ml) raw honey

¼ cup (56 g) brown sugar

Place the cocoa butter and chamomile-infused coconut oil in a heatproof jar or, for easy cleanup, an empty unlined soup can. Place the jar or can into a saucepan containing a few inches (7 cm) of water. Set the pan over a medium-low burner until the cocoa butter is melted.

Remove from heat and stir in the honey and brown sugar. Scoop the mixture into the sections of an ice cube tray, then place in the freezer until solid. Remove from the mold.

During summer and in warm climates, store the scrub cubes in a cool place or even your refrigerator to prevent melting.

Use 1 to 2 cubes during your shower or bath on dry, rough areas of skin that need exfoliating. These are especially effective on feet to help them get summer-sandal ready. Scrubs should generally be used only once every week or two, but if using on tough areas such as your feet, you can use them more often until you reach a level of smoothness you're happy with. Be careful as you exit the tub after using a scrub cube, since the cocoa butter and coconut oil can make the floor slippery.

DIY Lip Care

There's no need to spend a fortune on little tubes and jars of natural lip balms, glosses and scrubs from the store when you can make your own at home for far less!

Lip balm is probably one of the simplest DIY projects around and a fun activity for all ages. In this chapter, I share several of my favorite lip balm projects along with a couple of scrubs to help keep your lips smooth and flake-free.

Once you've tried your hand at making one of my recipes, you might want to jump in and create your own variations. I've got you covered with my detailed guide for making the perfect custom lip balm that's just right for you!

Favorite Herbal Lip Balms

While I've listed a few fun lip balm recipes, they represent only a tiny fraction of the potential recipe combinations to be created. After you've tried out one or two of my projects, flip to page 130 and try your hand at making your own custom lip balms from scratch!

The ingredients for each recipe are listed by weight. You'll get the best results by using a digital scale to measure them out. I realize, though, that some may not have access to a scale, which makes it difficult to follow the recipes closely. Here are a few volume equivalents that might help you approximate the recipes more easily:

➻ 1 tbsp of oil = about 10 to 12 grams

➻ 1 tbsp cosmetic butter = about 14 grams

➻ 1 tbsp tightly packed beeswax, grated or pastilles = about 10 grams

The directions for each lip balm are the same, so choose one that sounds good to you (pages 126–129), assemble the ingredients and follow the directions below.

To Make the Lip Balm or Tint

Combine the oil(s), butter (if using) and beeswax in a heatproof jar or container. For easy cleanup, you can use an empty, unlined tin can. If your recipe calls for alkanet root as a colorant, add it to the oils before heating.

Set the jar down into a saucepan that has 1 to 2 inches (2.5 to 5 cm) of water in the bottom, then place the pan over a medium-low burner until the wax is melted. Remove from heat, add essential oils, if desired, and pour into lip balm tubes or small tins.

Allow the lip balm to cool for several hours or until completely firm. Cap and store out of direct heat and sunlight. When stored properly, lip balm will stay fresh for around 6 to 9 months.

Classic Peppermint Lip Balm

Castor oil lends a slight glossy sheen and helps this minty fresh balm glide on smoothly, leaving lips feeling hydrated and refreshed.

YIELD: 12 TO 14 TUBES OF LIP BALM

1 oz (28 g) mint-infused sunflower oil
(see page 17 for how to infuse oil)

0.5 oz (14 g) castor oil

0.5 oz (14 g) beeswax

8 to 10 drops peppermint essential oil

Chocolate Mint Lip Balm

This lip balm has a yummy chocolate-mint flavor thanks to the addition of real chocolate chips and peppermint essential oil. Melt the chocolate chips in the same container and at the same time as you melt the beeswax and cocoa butter.

YIELD: 14 TO 16 TUBES OF LIP BALM

1.5 oz (42 g) mint-infused grapeseed oil
(see page 17 for how to infuse oil)

0.5 oz (14 g) cocoa butter

0.5 oz (14 g) beeswax

6 chocolate chips

10 to 12 drops peppermint essential oil

Basil & Lime Lip Balm

Basil is a terrific herb with anti-inflammatory and antiaging properties. Lime essential oil adds a sprightly flavor and scent, but double check that the brand you use is distilled, so that it doesn't cause your lips to be more sensitive to sun exposure.

YIELD: 12 TO 14 TUBES OF LIP BALM

1 oz (28 g) basil-infused olive oil
(see page 17 for how to infuse oil)

0.5 oz (14 g) castor oil

0.5 oz (14 g) beeswax

10 to 12 drops distilled lime essential oil

Favorite Herbal Lip Balms (continued)

Daisy Vanilla Lip Balm (1)

The common daisy has been studied and shown to have some quite remarkable healing properties. Use this balm on chapped or damaged lips. Vanilla absolute oil, which is not the same thing as vanilla extract, adds a nice bit of scent, but if you're unable to procure some, you can omit it or try another essential oil, such as peppermint.

YIELD: 14 TO 16 TUBES OF LIP BALM

1.5 oz (42 g) daisy-infused olive oil
(see page 17 for how to infuse oils)

0.5 oz (14 g) mango butter

0.5 oz (14 g) beeswax

10 to 12 drops vanilla absolute oil

Dandelion Plantain Chapped Lip Treatment (2)

Dandelion and plantain are two of the greatest skin-healing herbs around. The best part about them is that often they're available in your own yard, free for the picking! If you suffer from dry, chapped lips, try this recipe for soothing relief.

YIELD: 6 (0.5-OUNCE [14-G]) TINS

1 oz (28 g) dandelion-infused oil
(see page 17 for how to infuse oils)

1 oz (28 g) plantain-infused oil

0.5 oz (14 g) kokum butter

0.5 oz (14 g) castor oil

0.5 oz (14 g) beeswax

10 to 12 drops peppermint essential oil

Rosy Lip Tint (3)

Alkanet root provides the rosy red color in this lip balm that appears dark in the tin, but shows up as a sheer pale pink when rubbed over your lips. You can adjust the amount of alkanet root at will for lighter or darker shades of pink or red.

YIELD: 4 (0.5-OUNCE [14-G]) TINS

1.5 oz (42 g) rose-infused oil
(see page 17 for how to infuse oils)

0.5 oz (14 g) castor oil

0.5 oz (14 g) beeswax

1/8 tsp alkanet root

Vegan Sunflower Lip Tint

Sunflower wax is colorless, resulting in a pure white lip balm that takes color nicely. In keeping with the sunflower theme and because of its terrific skin conditioning properties, I used sunflower-infused sunflower oil in this recipe.

YIELD: 2 (0.5-OUNCE [14-G]) TINS

0.65 oz (19 g) shea butter

0.15 oz (4 g) sunflower wax

0.5 oz (14 g) sunflower-infused sunflower oil
(see page 17 for how to infuse oils)

1/8 tsp alkanet root

Create Your Own Lip Balm

Homemade lip balm is so easy to make and so much better than store bought! By learning just one basic formula, you can create an almost unlimited variety of personalized lip balms and glosses. They make wonderful gifts to share with friends and family as well!

This basic formula is the cornerstone of every lip balm recipe that I make. It helps nourish and protect the delicate skin found on our lips and keeps them feeling hydrated and smooth. Be sure to read on past the recipe instructions for the helpful sections on customizing your lip balm further with herbs, essential oils, natural colorants and honey.

YIELD: APPROXIMATELY 12 TO 16 TUBES OF LIP BALM

1.5 oz (43 g) oil, infused or plain (see page 17 for how to infuse oils)

0.5 oz (14 g) shea, mango or avocado butter (optional)

0.5 oz (14 g) beeswax

8 to 12 drops essential oil (optional)

Tip: If the lip balm is intended for use in jars or metal tins instead of tubes, add another ounce (14 g) of oil for a softer consistency that can be applied more easily with your finger.

Variation: For a vegan option, use approximately 8 to 10 grams of candelilla wax or 6 to 8 grams of sunflower wax instead of beeswax.

Combine your chosen oil(s), butter (if using) and beeswax in a canning jar, unlined tin can or other heatproof container.

Shea, mango or avocado butter are soft enough that you can add them to the recipe, if you'd like, without them adversely affecting the ratios of oil to wax. However, if you decide to use a hard butter such as cocoa or kokum instead, you may need to add 3 or 4 extra grams of oil to compensate for the extra firmness they bring to lip balm.

Set the jar or container down into a saucepan that has 1 to 2 inches (2.5 to 5 cm) of water in the bottom. Place the pan over a medium-low burner until the wax is melted. Remove from heat, add essential oils, if desired, and pour into lip balm tubes or small tins.

Allow the lip balm to cool for several hours or until completely firm. If you find that your lip balm is too soft, you can melt it back into a liquid state and add a little more beeswax. Conversely, if your lip balm is too firm, you can melt it again and add more oil.

Cap and store the finished product out of direct heat and sunlight. The shelf life of lip balm depends on the quality and age of the ingredients that you start with. Older oils will go rancid more quickly, but homemade lip balm usually stays fresh for around 6 to 9 months.

Customizing Your Lip Balm Recipes

Some garden herbs and flowers are more suited to lip balms than others.

A FEW HERBS AND FLOWERS TO CONSIDER INFUSING IN OIL FOR USE IN YOUR LIP BALM CREATIONS

Basil—skin repairing

Calendula—healing

Chamomile—anti-inflammatory

Daisy—heals damaged skin

Dandelion Flowers—for cracked, chapped skin

Lemon Balm—fights the virus that causes cold sores

Plantain—for chapped lips

Mint—lightly scents oil

Rose—soothing

Sunflower Petals—skin conditioning

Violet Leaf—for flaky, dry lips

SOME OILS THAT DO WELL IN LIP BALM

Apricot Oil—for sensitive or mature skin

Avocado Oil—nourishing

Castor Oil—highly recommended, adds gloss and smoothness

Coconut Oil—melts easily, so counts as an oil instead of solid butter

Grapeseed Oil—light, absorbs quickly

Hemp Seed Oil—nutritious

Olive Oil—all-purpose, easy to find

Sunflower Oil—light, heals damaged skin

Sweet Almond Oil—softens lips

Tamanu Oil—helps a variety of skin conditions

While they're an optional component, cosmetic butters can enrich your recipe and help your lip balm to stay on longer. Shea, mango or avocado butter are soft enough that you can add them to the recipe, if you'd like, without them adversely affecting the ratios of oil to wax. However, if you decide to use a hard butter such as cocoa or kokum instead, you may need to add 3 or 4 extra grams of oil to compensate for the extra firmness they bring to lip balm.

SOME GOOD BUTTER CHOICES

Cocoa Butter—rich and creamy, protects skin

Kokum Butter—for dry, cracked skin, a good substitute for cocoa butter

Shea Butter—for weathered, dry skin, unrefined tends to have a distinctive smell

Mango Butter—moisturizes and softens, can be exchanged for shea butter

Avocado Butter—wonderfully smooth and nourishing, suitable for those with tree nut allergies

(continued)

Adding Colors and Essential Oils to Lip Balms

Since lip balms contain oils and no water, they should be colored with oil-soluble colorants such as:

Alkanet Root—use a tiny pinch to get colors ranging from pink to dark red

Annatto Seed—for shades of orange

Chlorella—for a pale shade of lime green

For best results, infuse your oil with the natural colorant a few days ahead of time, then strain through a cheese cloth before using. This keeps little specks from appearing in your balm.

Colored clays are not recommended, since they may pull moisture from your lips and dry them out.

The judicious use of essential oils can add a delightful scent to your lip balm. In some ways they act as a light flavoring, too, but not like the candy-flavored lip balms you may remember from your youth. Cold-pressed lemon and lime oils are phototoxic, which means they can make you more prone to sunburn if you apply them before outdoor activities; however, distilled versions are available and are safer to use.

- Lemon—distilled only
- Lime—distilled only
- Mandarin
- Tangerine
- Sweet Orange
- Peppermint
- Rose
- Spearmint
- Vanilla Absolute

For a hint of chocolate, try stirring in a pinch of unsweetened cocoa powder, unrefined cocoa butter or a few chocolate chips into the melted lip balm before pouring into tubes or tins.

Adding Honey to Lip Balm

Lip balm is a naturally anhydrous product. That means it contains all oil and no water. Honey, however, is a water-based product. While we know that water and oil won't readily mix, it is possible to make a lip balm with honey, with a few caveats.

After melting your lip balm ingredients, remove from heat and stir in the honey while it's still hot. For the lip balm formula given in this book, you can try adding around $1/4$ teaspoon honey. Stir continuously for about 2 minutes, then let the mixture sit until it starts to firm up. Stir again for 2 to 3 more minutes and spoon into tubes or small jars. The extra stirring will help the honey better incorporate into the lip balm, though over time, it will still tend to bead out. Don't store a honey-containing lip balm in tins, since any type of water-based ingredient could make them rust.

Chamomile Lip Scrub

Winter weather and heated indoor air can play havoc on skin, hair and lips. Use this gentle scrub, once every week or two, followed by a nourishing lip balm, to remedy dry, flaky lips. Chamomile was chosen for this recipe because of its ability to soothe and relieve irritation and inflammation. Sunflower is excellent for repairing broken skin, but other oils that work well in this recipe include olive, sweet almond, rosehip, jojoba, hemp and avocado.

YIELD: ¼ CUP (60 ML) OF LIP SCRUB

2 tbsp (30 ml) sunflower oil

1 tbsp (1 g) dried chamomile flowers

2 tbsp (26 g) granulated sugar

Using one of the methods on page 17, infuse the sunflower oil with the chamomile flowers. Strain the finished oil.

Combine the sugar and infused oil and stir well. Spoon into a glass jar. Store in a cool location, out of direct sunlight.

To use, rub a small amount over dry, flaky lips with your finger. Be light-handed and gentle as the skin on your lips is very thin and sensitive. Although the ingredients are technically edible and won't harm you if licked, this recipe isn't intended for consumption. Rinse the scrub off with warm water and follow with a handmade, moisturizing lip balm from earlier in the chapter.

Mint Lip Scrub

This naturally colored lip scrub is a delightful way to use mint from the garden. Common white sugar is a brilliant exfoliant that works to polish away dry, flaky skin. It's paired here with nourishing sweet almond oil to help soften and condition your lips. If you're allergic to almonds or other tree nuts, try olive, sunflower or avocado oil instead. Because scrubs are intensive treatments and lips are delicate, it's best to use this scrub only once every week or two, followed by a moisturizing lip balm, for softer, smoother lips.

YIELD: 3 TABLESPOONS (37 G) MINT LIP SCRUB

2 tbsp (26 g) granulated sugar

2 to 3 fresh mint leaves, chopped

1 tbsp (15 ml) sweet almond oil

Using a small food processor, blend the sugar and mint leaves until finely ground and evenly mixed. Spread the sugar out over a sheet of wax paper to dry for 1 to 2 days. The sugar will retain a fresh green color, even when dried. If needed, run the mint sugar through the food processor once more to smooth out any clumps before proceeding with the recipe.

Combine the sugar and oil together in a small jar.

To use, rub a small amount over dry, flaky lips with your finger. Be light-handed and gentle, as the skin on your lips is very thin and sensitive. Although the ingredients are technically edible and won't harm you if licked, this recipe isn't intended for consumption. Rinse the scrub off with warm water and follow with a handmade, moisturizing lip balm from earlier in the chapter.

Tip: Mix up extra mint sugar when fresh mint is in season to use later in the year for both cosmetic and food use. Mint sugar is wonderful in tea, on toast and sprinkled on muffins!

Luscious Hair Care

Shiny, beautiful hair starts from the inside, with a healthy diet and lifestyle, and is further helped with regular trims and haircuts. In spite of our best efforts, though, daily exposure to blow dryers, flatirons, pool water and the sun can all play havoc on our locks.

Before you drop a lot of money into expensive products to repair and care for your hair, try some of these recipes made from easy-to-find, all-natural ingredients, such as honey, coconut oil and vinegar, coupled with beneficial herbs and flowers straight from your backyard.

If your hair is damaged and in need of an intense repair, be sure to check out Hollyhock Split-End Crème (page 141), Nettle, Coconut & Honey Hair Mask (page 142) or Sunflower Hot Oil Treatment (page 144). Dry, flaky scalps will benefit from the dandruff-busting thyme spray or a customized calendula and catnip hair rinse.

In this chapter, I'll also show you how to make your own custom herbal shampoos that are just right for your hair type!

Hollyhock Split-End Crème

The only true way to get rid of existing split ends is by trimming them off; however, this crème can help smooth things out between haircuts. Argan oil is well known for its remarkable properties that nourish, strengthen, protect and add shine to hair, though it's on the pricy side. If it's not in your budget, try using coconut or olive oil instead. Hollyhocks were chosen for this recipe because they smooth and moisturize, but other good choices include sunflower and nettle. Aloe vera gel makes this crème lighter and easier to wash out, while vitamin-rich shea butter helps bind everything together in a wax-free way. It's important to remember with this hair crème that you only need the tiniest bit to be effective!

YIELD: ALMOST FILLS A 2-OUNCE (60-ML) GLASS JAR

2 tbsp (30 ml) argan oil

1 tbsp (1 g) crumbled dried hollyhock leaves or flowers

1 tbsp (14 g) shea butter

1 tbsp (15 ml) aloe vera gel

2 to 3 drops of your favorite essential oil (optional)

Natural preservative (optional)

Infuse the argan oil with hollyhocks using one of the methods on page 17. Strain the finished oil before proceeding with the recipe.

In a small jar or heatproof container, melt the shea butter by placing the jar or container in a small saucepan of hot water. Once melted, combine it with the hollyhock-infused oil.

Place the mixture in the refrigerator for around 30 minutes or until it starts to firm up. Using a fork, stir well. Add the aloe, then stir vigorously for about 2 minutes. The mixture will start to turn opaque and creamy. If you are adding essential oil or a natural preservative, do so at this time. Set the mixture aside for 5 minutes to thicken, then stir thoroughly once more with the fork. You should now have a thickened cream.

To use, dab a very small amount on your fingertips. Working with one section of hair at a time, lightly rub the crème into just the ends. Depending on your hair type, it will take the crème anywhere from 30 minutes to several hours to soak in, leaving the tips shiny and healthy looking. If they look greasy instead, that means you used a little too much, so go lighter next time.

If you don't use a preservative, store the crème in a cool place and use within a few weeks.

Nettle, Coconut & Honey Hair Mask

This mask is superpowered with nettle for its ability to promote strong, shiny and healthy hair. Coconut oil is an excellent treatment for damaged hair, but if you're allergic, try using babassu oil instead for a similar effect. Raw honey might sound like an odd (and sticky!) ingredient to put on your hair, but it helps to gently clean and moisturize hair, leaving it frizz free in the process.

YIELD: ABOUT 12 TO 24 APPLICATIONS, DEPENDING ON HAIR LENGTH AND CONDITION

¼ cup (3 g) dried nettle leaves

½ cup (100 g) unrefined coconut oil

Raw honey, as needed

Infuse the coconut oil with nettle, using the Quick Method on page 17. Strain. The infused oil should be stored out of direct sunlight and heat in between uses. The shelf life is around 9 to 12 months.

Mix up small batches of this mask, as needed, using equal parts of nettle-infused coconut oil and raw honey. Try starting with 1 teaspoon of coconut oil and 1 teaspoon of honey. Stir together until blended. Use more or less depending on your hair length, texture and level of damage.

When you first get in the shower, wet your hair thoroughly with water. Apply the mask to the ends of the hair, avoiding the scalp unless it's dry and flaky. Leave on for 5 to 10 minutes while you finish your shower. Shampoo the mask out and rinse well.

How often you use this mask is highly individualized. Some hair types may benefit from more frequent use, once or twice per week, while others may find the need to use it only once every month or two. Experiment to find the schedule that's right for you.

Thyme Flaky Scalp Spray

An itchy, flaky scalp is more than a cosmetic nuisance; it can be downright uncomfortable to live with. Antifungal thyme is a top choice for cleansing the scalp and treating dandruff, while honey reduces flakes and helps retain moisture. Apple cider vinegar works to restore pH and leaves hair shinier and healthier looking. Use this spray after each shampoo and your scalp should show considerable improvement after a few weeks. If you don't find relief by then, investigate further; you may be reacting to an ingredient in your shampoo or something in your diet.

YIELD: 1/2 CUP (120 ML)

1/4 cup (1 g) chopped thyme, dry or fresh

1/2 cup (120 ml) apple cider vinegar

1 tsp raw honey

Place the thyme and apple cider vinegar in a half-pint (250-ml) canning jar. Set it aside for at least 2 to 3 days to infuse. Strain, then stir in the honey.

Pour the thyme vinegar and honey into a spray bottle.

To use, spray on your scalp after shampooing, lifting your hair as needed in order to saturate as much area as possible. Be careful not to spray into your eyes. If you inadvertently do, just rinse them thoroughly with water for several minutes. Massage the spray into your scalp for a short bit and then rinse out with water.

Variation: If thyme isn't available, calendula, lavender, mint, rosemary and sage are other good antidandruff choices.

Sunflower Hot Oil Treatment

Instead of spending a lot of money on tiny packets of store-bought hot oil treatments, you can easily make your own at home. Sunflower petal extract is sometimes added to high-end hair care products for its ability to condition and add shine, making sunflowers a natural choice for us to use in this recipe as well. Jojoba is an outstanding oil added for its nourishing and hair-strengthening properties, but if it's out of your price range or not available, try coconut, olive or sunflower oil instead.

YIELD: ½ CUP (120 ML)

½ cup (120 ml) jojoba oil

¼ cup (5 g) dried sunflower petals

Infuse the jojoba oil with sunflowers, using one of the methods on page 17. Strain the finished oil and proceed with the recipe.

To use, pour a small amount of infused oil into a cup or jar. Set the cup down into a bowl of very hot (but not boiling) water for 5 minutes or until the oil is warmed. Massage the warm oil into your hair, starting with the tips. If you feel you need it, you can work the oil further up your hair. Unless your scalp is incredibly dry or flaky though, you may want to stop when you get a few inches away from your roots, to avoid excessive oiliness.

The amount you use will vary greatly depending on hair type and length, but a ballpark starting amount is ½ teaspoon of oil for short hair and 1 teaspoon for long hair. Leave on for 5 to 10 minutes, then shampoo out.

For a deeper treatment, apply the oil to your hair as directed above, then wrap it up in a towel. Leave the oil on for 30 minutes to 1 hour before shampooing out.

Infused oils, such as this sunflower hot oil treatment, have a shelf life of 9 to 12 months, when stored out of direct heat and sunlight.

Herbal Dry Shampoo

Dry shampoos are a great solution for those days that you wake up late or don't have time to wash your hair. The key ingredient for this recipe is arrowroot powder or cornstarch, both of which help absorb excess oil. When used alone, they can leave a light layer of white powder behind, so I've created three recipes designed for light, medium and dark hair. Each dry shampoo formula includes one or more herbal powders for their scalp benefits or use as a subtle colorant. To make an herbal or floral powder, grind dried herbs or flowers in a coffee grinder, then sift them through a fine mesh sieve to yield a soft, silky powder. A general guideline is to grind around ¼ cup (60 ml) of dried herbs to yield roughly 1 tablespoon (4 g) of powder.

The light hair tones variation incorporates powdered calendula flowers for their scalp-toning properties and to break up the stark white color of the arrowroot.

Cocoa powder adds a brown tint to the medium hair tones dry shampoo while powdered hibiscus (or red rose) flowers add a hint of red.

Dark hair types need the extra cocoa in the dark tones variation in order to help the dry shampoo blend into your hair color. I added nettle leaves, too, for their hair-strengthening benefits and darker color. As an alternative, try using ground rosemary instead.

YIELD: ½ CUP (65 G) DRY SHAMPOO

LIGHT HAIR TONES FORMULA

1 tbsp (4 g) powdered calendula flowers

½ cup (65 g) arrowroot powder

MEDIUM HAIR TONES FORMULA

3 tbsp (18 g) cocoa powder

2 tbsp (7 g) powdered hibiscus flowers or red rose petals

½ cup (65 g) arrowroot powder

DARK HAIR TONES FORMULA

2 tbsp (7 g) powdered nettle leaves

½ cup (65 g) arrowroot powder

5 tbsp (30 g) cocoa powder

Combine all of the ingredients in a bowl or jar. To use, sprinkle a small amount onto the crown of your head. Start out with just a bit, since you can always add more. Work the powder into your roots, using your fingers. Brush out with a hairbrush, until no sign of the shampoo is left.

Create Your Own Herbal Shampoo

This recipe features liquid castile soap, which can be found in most health stores. Combined with an herbal tea, a small amount of moisturizing oil and essential oils for scent, it makes an effective shampoo for many hair types. Because of the high alkalinity, this shampoo is not recommended for color-treated hair, as it may strip away dye. It has, however, been successfully used on henna-treated hair.

YIELD: 6 OUNCES (180 ML) SHAMPOO

Dried or fresh herbs and flowers

4 to 5 oz (120 to 150 ml) simmering water

2 oz (60 ml) liquid castile soap

¼ tsp sunflower, olive, jojoba or another light oil

20 to 40 drops essential oil

Natural preservative (optional)

Vinegar hair rinse (see page 150)

It's essential to follow up with a vinegar hair rinse (page 150) after shampooing, to restore pH and remove shampoo residue. Some, especially those with hard water or fine hair, may find this shampoo weighs down their hair too much. If you try it out and don't care for the result, use the rest as a body wash and try out shampoo bars (pages 174 and 177) instead!

Look through the flower and herb descriptions on pages 8 to 15 and choose one or more herbs. Some good choices include: moisturizing hollyhock, shine-promoting sunflower, rosemary for thinning hair, lavender or chamomile for itchy scalp, calendula for chronic scalp conditions, thyme or sage for dandruff, roses for oily scalp, violets for dry scalp and nettle to stimulate hair growth.

Fill a half-pint (250-ml) jar about halfway with your chosen herb(s) and flower(s). Pour the simmering water over the herbs and flowers in the jar. Stir them around for a few seconds, to make sure they're covered in the water, then let them steep for around 1 hour. Strain.

Gently stir the castile soap and sunflower oil into the infused water.

Choose an essential oil for your shampoo. Some you may want to consider include: lavender (relieves dry scalp), peppermint (refreshing), rose (toning), tea tree (for dandruff) or rosemary (antimicrobial). If you're pregnant, nursing or have chronic health conditions, check with your health care provider before using essential oils.

Add around 20 or more drops of your chosen essential oil into the shampoo.

This homemade shampoo will stay fresh for around 1 week, if stored in your refrigerator between uses. To extend shelf life, add a natural preservative (see page 26).

To use, shake well and pour a small amount of herbal shampoo into the palm of your hand. It's normal for it to look thin and watery. Rub the shampoo between your fingers and palms to work up some lather. Massage the lather into your scalp and partially down your hair. There's no need to focus on the ends, as the process of rinsing should sufficiently clean them. Rinse well under running water, then follow with a vinegar rinse or spray (page 150).

⇢   See picture on page 138.

Rosemary Beard Oil

This beard oil conditions and tames unruly and itchy beards. By increasing circulation, rosemary stimulates hair growth and improves its overall health. If rosemary isn't available, try using dried lavender leaves or pine needles instead. Olive oil was chosen for this recipe since it's a great all-purpose emollient that works for most skin and hair types. Other good choices include sunflower, argan, apricot, grapeseed or sweet almond oil. You can even blend together more than one type of oil, if you'd like, to customize this recipe further. The tea tree oil is optional, but will help if itching or flakiness is a problem.

YIELD: ½ CUP (120 ML) BEARD OIL

½ cup (120 ml) olive oil

3 tbsp (2 g) dried rosemary

Drop or two of tea tree oil (optional)

Infuse the olive oil with dried rosemary, using one of the methods on page 17.

For a stronger scent and more powerful herbal action, pour the freshly strained oil over a new batch of dried rosemary and repeat the process to create a double-infused oil.

Use your fingers to rub a small amount of oil into your beard, as needed. Shelf life is around 9 months or longer, depending on type of oil used.

Create Your Own Vinegar Hair Rinse

After-shampoo vinegar rinses are an important part of using homemade shampoos and shampoo bars. They help restore pH, remove shampoo residue, soften hair and can be beneficial for flaky or irritated scalp conditions. While several types of vinegars are available and have similar effect on the hair, apple cider vinegar is preferred because it's less processed and contains more nutrients than standard white vinegar.

Use the following formula to custom-tailor a vinegar hair rinse specifically suited to your hair type. If you don't have fresh plants on hand, you can use half as much dried instead.

YIELD: ABOUT 8 APPLICATIONS (10 CUPS [2.4 L])

2 cups (500 ml) apple cider vinegar

1 cup (15 to 20 g) coarsely chopped fresh herbs or flowers

8 cups (1.9 L) water

Infuse the vinegar and herbs for two weeks, then strain.

To make the hair rinse, combine ¼ cup (60 ml) of vinegar with 1 cup (250 ml) of water. Depending on your hair type, you may want to adjust the ratios of vinegar and water to make the rinse stronger or milder.

Pour the diluted rinse over your hair and scalp after shampooing. There's no need to rinse, though you can if you'd like.

For a more convenient alternative, you can fill a small spray bottle with the undiluted infused vinegar and store it in your shower. Spritz it all over your scalp and hair after shampooing, then follow with a rinse of plain water.

Herbs and flowers to consider using in your hair rinse include:

Basil—antimicrobial

Calendula—soothes scalp

Catnip—for flaky scalp

Chamomile—reputed to lighten blond hair

Mint—increases scalp circulation

Nettle—stimulates hair growth

Roses—uplifting and soothing

Rosemary—improves scalp circulation

Sage—cleansing

Sunflower—makes hair shiny

Thyme—antiseptic

Violets—soothes and won't strip moisture

Simple Homemade Soaps

Many people are interested in making their own soap, but begin to feel intimidated or overwhelmed once they start researching the craft. I know, because I was the same way for a long time!

Once I made my first successful batch, though, I realized that the hardest part of soap making is just gathering up the bravery to actually try it. Yes, you do have to follow certain safety rules, but if you take your time and work carefully and methodically, it's not difficult.

The most rewarding part about soap making for me was being able to make my sensitive and highly allergic toddler a soap that cleared his eczema and left his rough, dry skin so smooth that his doctor was beyond impressed. That's an empowering feeling that money just can't buy.

In this chapter, I'll take beginners step-by-step through the basics of soap making. Once you're familiar with the process, try making a batch of Chamomile "Almost Castile" Soap (page 162). It's a simple recipe that requires just two oils and makes a lovely, gentle soap that's wonderful for all skin types. If you don't have chamomile on hand, don't worry, I have plenty of substitution ideas for you!

Veteran soap makers will enjoy perusing the recipe section, filled with nourishing and healing soaps such as Thyme & Witch Hazel Clear Skin Facial Bar (page 171) and Carrot & Calendula Soap (page 182).

Shampoo bars are a popular item to make and give, so I've included two of my favorites here as well, featuring sunflowers and hollyhocks, two flowers that can help smooth hair and leave it shiny and healthy looking.

I wrap up the chapter with an easy-to-make, pure coconut oil soap that works fantastic as a stain stick and laundry detergent!

Soap Making Basics

Before you jump into the process of making soap, there are a few things to know.

In order to make soap, you need to combine a caustic substance with oils or fat. In days past, our grandmothers used potash, made from wood ashes and animal fats. The problem was that there was no way to know how strong or weak the potash was and how much fat should be used in ratio to it. The result was often a harsh bar that did well for cleaning laundry, but didn't feel so great on skin!

Today, we have one standardized chemical for making bar soap. It's called sodium hydroxide, or more commonly, lye. Because it never changes, we can use online lye calculators and figure out exactly how much we need to make a perfectly balanced bar of soap every single time.

In order to do this, it's important that all ingredients, even water and oils, are measured by weight instead of volume, since inconsistent measurements will yield unreliable results.

Some people fear that because lye is a caustic substance, some might be leftover in the soap and will hurt your skin. That's an understandable concern, but it's completely untrue. Every single molecule of lye reacts with corresponding molecules of oil and they both turn into something new—soap plus glycerin. There is no lye left in a properly made bar of soap.

Store-bought soaps either contain chemical detergents or lye. Look on the label of your favorite soap. If it has the words "saponified," "sodium cocoate," "sodium tallowate" or "sodium palmitate," that's just another way of saying oils that have been reacted with sodium hydroxide, or lye.

Lye is a strong chemical that does require utmost caution and respect when handling. For safety, wear a pair of goggles, to protect your eyes from splashes, along with rubber or latex gloves and long sleeves.

Always add lye to liquids, and not the other way around, or it may have a volcano effect and make a mess. When mixing lye into water or another liquid, it gets very hot fast, and strong fumes will develop for a few moments. Don't breathe these fumes in directly. The ideal place to work is in your kitchen sink, with the window open for fresh air.

Handling lye is for grownups only. Make sure small children and pets are out of the area. Lye solutions should be clearly marked with both words and danger symbols for nonreaders.

If you get lye on your skin, rinse repeatedly with copious amounts of cool water. For large-area burns or if you get it in your eyes, rinse and seek medical attention right away.

I know that all of these safety warnings make lye sound pretty scary! Keep in mind, though, that soap is made every day by many people without incident. If you can safely handle bleach, another potentially harmful chemical, you should be able to handle lye with the same amount of competence.

Soap Making Equipment

There are a few basic things you'll need for making soap.

Digital Scale—it's important that soap-making ingredients, especially the lye, are measured precisely in order to make a balanced bar of soap. An accurate digital scale is a must. Check at your local big-box store, near the kitchen accessories section, for a reasonably priced one.

Thermometer—a candy thermometer works well to measure the temperature of lye solution and oils. Save it just for soap making, though, and get a separate one for making candy.

Small Measuring Container—this is for measuring dry lye. Mark it clearly with the words "LYE" and a symbol for nonreaders. I use a plastic cup.

Heatproof Pitcher—for mixing the lye and water together. Use stainless steel or heavy-duty plastic. Some people use heatproof glass, but over time the inside develops weaknesses that make it prone to breakage, so it's not recommended.

Soap Pot or Large Bowl—for mixing the whole thing together. It should be stainless steel, high-density plastic, enamel-lined or ceramic. Don't use aluminum or nonstick surfaces; they will react badly with lye.

Heatproof Mixing Utensils—use heavy-duty plastic or silicone spoons and spatulas for mixing and scraping soap into the mold.

Rubber Gloves, Long Sleeves and Safety Goggles—to keep hands, arms and eyes protected.

Stick or Immersion Blender—shortens stirring time considerably and is highly recommended. Don't use a regular handheld mixer with beaters; it doesn't work in the same way.

Soap Molds—you can buy a 3-pound (1.3-kg) mold for the recipes in this book, or use a glass loaf pan, like the kind you make bread in, and line it with parchment paper or an inexpensive trash bag. A similarly lined, sturdy small shoebox or plastic storage container could work too.

Lining Molds

This is a step that can be done several ways. One method is to use two long sheets of parchment or freezer paper, one cut to the exact width of the mold and the other cut to the exact length. Lay the sheets across each other so they hang over the sides of the mold. This makes it easy to lift the finished soap out of the mold by the paper.

For a quick and easy liner, buy a bag of unscented store-brand trash bags. Make sure they're not the thinnest, flimsy kind that tears easily, but they don't have to be expensive either. Open the bag and press it to fit neatly into the bottom of the mold. You'll find that you have a lot of bag left over when you're done. You can tie it up, out of the way, or trim the excess off.

You can bypass the need for lining your mold in the first place by buying silicone molds or wooden ones with silicone liners. While they have the advantage of being nonstick, they often hold in moisture longer, so your soaps may have to sit in them a few extra days before they can be unmolded.

Unmolding & Slicing Bars of Soap

Soap can often be unmolded 24 to 48 hours after being poured into the mold. It should be completely cool and feel solid when pressed. Some silicone molds or very deep ones will hold in moisture longer, so may take several extra days before the soap is firm enough to unmold easily. If you continually have problems with unmolding soap, try reducing the water in your recipe by 0.5 ounce (14 grams) or adding around 1½ teaspoons (7.5 ml) of sodium lactate (a salt, naturally derived from corn or beets). Both of these techniques will help the soap harden faster.

Once your soap is firm enough, remove it from the mold and place the loaf on a sheet of parchment or wax paper. Slice evenly into bars using a soap cutter or sharp, unserrated knife. How thick you slice the bars is a personal preference, but many soap makers like to cut them about 1 to 1¼ inch (2.5 to 3 cm) thick.

Adding Natural Fragrance and Color

Essential oils can be added to soap for natural fragrance, though it does take a fairly significant amount, around 2 tablespoons (30 ml) per batch, to create a noticeable, long-lasting scent. (Use half as much for a lighter scent.) If you plan on scenting your soaps with essential oils, you'll find that online vendors of soap supplies are significantly more economical than local health stores, where tiny bottles are often expensive. Many citrus essential-oil scents fade too quickly, while other essential oils are too cost prohibitive to use in soap. Some that I've found to work well include lavender, rose geranium, peppermint, spearmint, lime, 10x (ten-fold) orange, lemongrass and eucalyptus.

To color soap naturally, try adding clays and botanicals, such as annatto seed powder (for yellow and orange), purple Brazilian clay, French green clay, rose kaolin clay and indigo powder.

Soap Making Overview

Now that you have the basics down, you're ready to make soap! Remember that all measurements are by weight, even the water portion.

STEP 1

Assemble your ingredients and don your safety gear of gloves, goggles and long sleeves. I like to lay several sheets of wax paper over my work area, to make cleanup easier. Prepare your mold by lining it, unless it's silicone. (See page 157.)

STEP 2

Weigh out the water or herbal tea part of the recipe into a heatproof container and set it down into your kitchen sink or other spot near a source of fresh air. Weigh out the lye in a separate container.

STEP 3

Pour the lye into the water or tea and stir gently with a heatproof spatula or spoon until the lye is fully dissolved from the bottom of the container. Always add the lye to water and not the other way around, to avoid a potentially dangerous, and messy, lye-volcano. Avoid directly breathing in the strong fumes. Set the solution aside in a safe place out of reach of children and pets, and let cool for about 30 to 40 minutes. The temperature should drop to around 100 to 110°F (38 to 43°C) during that time.

STEP 4

While the lye solution is cooling, weigh out the oils and butters you'll need for your recipe. Melt coconut oil and any solid butters in a double boiler before adding to the other oils in your bigger soap-making pot or mixing container. Heat the oils more, if necessary, until they're about 90 to 100°F (32 to 38°C).

STEP 5

Pour the lye solution into the pot or mixing container of oils. Hand stir with an immersion blender (powered off) for about 30 seconds, then turn the immersion blender on and mix the soap batter, alternating every 30 seconds or so with hand stirring to prevent the immersion blender's motor from burning out. Continue mixing until trace is reached. This could take anywhere from 2 to 10 minutes. "Trace" means that the soap batter is thick enough to leave a faint, fleeting imprint when it's drizzled across itself.

STEP 6

Once you've reached trace, you can choose to make either cold process soap or hot process soap.

(continued)

Soap Making Overview (continued)

For Cold Process Soap (1a)

Stir in any extra ingredients, such as essential oils, oatmeal, honey and such, then pour the soap batter into the prepared mold. At this stage, the soap is still caustic, so be sure to have your gloves on while handling it. Cover the mold with a sheet of wax paper and then the mold's top or a piece of cardboard. To retain heat, tuck a quilt or towel around it. Make sure it's in an area where it won't get disturbed or knocked over, then allow it to stay in the mold for 24 to 48 hours. After that time, remove the soap from the mold and slice into bars. Let the bars cure in the open air on sheets of wax paper or a coated baking rack for at least four weeks before using.

For Hot Process Soap (1b–5)

Pour the soap batter into a slow cooker turned on low heat. Cover with the lid and let cook for 1 hour, checking and stirring every 15 minutes. The soap will go through many changes during the process. At times, it will rise up higher and then fall back in on itself. Parts of the soap will turn dark and gel-like. This is all normal. After 1 hour of cook time has passed, give the soap a final stir. It will have a thickened consistency reminiscent of mashed potatoes. At this stage, stir in any extras such as essential oils, oatmeal, honey and such. Spoon the cooked soap into the prepared mold. Allow it to firm up overnight, then remove from the mold and slice into bars. You can use hot process soap bars right away, though it makes a longer lasting bar if it cures in the open air for a few weeks.

Chamomile "Almost Castile" Soap

This is a great recipe for a beginner since it only contains two oils. Traditional castile is a gentle, mild, 100 percent olive oil soap, with a low, creamy lather. By adding a small amount of castor oil to the recipe, we boost the bubbles while still retaining the mildness that makes castile perfect for those with supersensitive skin. I chose chamomile for this recipe because it calms and soothes rashes and other irritated skin conditions. If you don't have chamomile flowers or tea, try using lavender, rose, plantain, violet or calendula instead.

YIELD: 7 TO 8 BARS OF SOAP

¼ cup (4 g) dried chamomile flowers or 2 chamomile tea bags

10 oz (284 g) simmering water

3.7 oz (105 g) sodium hydroxide (lye)

26 oz (737 g) chamomile-infused olive oil (see page 17 for how to infuse oils)

3 oz (85 g) castor oil

FOR THE CHAMOMILE TEA

Place the dried chamomile flowers or tea bags in a heatproof jar or pitcher. Pour the simmering hot water over the flowers and let steep until the tea cools to room temperature. Strain.

FOR THE CHAMOMILE SOAP

Wearing protective gloves and eyewear, carefully stir the lye into the cooled chamomile tea. The tea will turn from light yellow to bright orange, which is a normal reaction. Set the solution aside in a safe place out of reach of children and pets and let cool for about 30 to 40 minutes. The temperature should drop to around 100 to 110°F (38 to 43°C) during that time.

While the lye solution is cooling, gently heat the chamomile-infused oil until it's about 90 to 100°F (32 to 38°C). Add the castor oil. Pour the warmed oils into your soap-making pot or bowl, then add the cooled lye solution.

Hand stir with an immersion blender (powered off) for about 30 seconds, then turn the immersion blender on and mix the soap batter, alternating every 30 seconds or so with hand stirring to prevent the immersion blender's motor from burning out. Continue mixing until trace is reached. Because this soap is high in olive oil, it may take up to 10 minutes to reach trace. "Trace" means that the soap batter is thick enough to leave a faint, fleeting imprint when it's drizzled across itself.

(continued)

FOR COLD PROCESS SOAP

Pour the soap into a prepared mold. Cover with a sheet of wax paper, then the mold's lid or a piece of cardboard. Tuck a towel or quilt around the mold to help it retain heat. Let it stay in the mold for 24 to 48 hours, then remove and slice into bars. Soaps that are high in olive oil take a little longer to firm up and cure than other types of soap, so these bars will give you the best result if you let them cure for at least 6 weeks before using.

FOR HOT PROCESS SOAP

Pour the soap batter into a slow cooker turned on low heat. Cover with the lid and let cook for 1 hour, checking and stirring every 15 minutes. After the final stir, spoon the cooked soap batter into a prepared mold. Allow it to firm up overnight, then remove from the mold and slice into bars. You can use the hot process soap right away, though it makes a longer lasting bar if it cures in the open air for a few weeks.

Variation: Castor oil was chosen for this recipe because it's a great way to boost bubbles in an otherwise low-lathering soap. If you don't have a way to get castor oil, though, you can use 3 ounces (85 g) of one of the following as a direct substitute for castor, with no other changes needed: cocoa butter (hardens soap), sweet almond oil (skin nourishing) or lard (hardens soap). If you use a substitute, keep in mind that your soap will still gently clean, it just might not lather as much.

Lavender Oatmeal Soap

Calming lavender is paired with soothing oats in this classic bar that's well suited for those with dry, sensitive or itchy skin. Sweet almond oil is added for its ability to nourish skin, while coconut oil hardens the bar and contributes to lots of bubbles. Olive oil, a fantastic emollient that helps soften skin, rounds out the trio of oils in this recipe. Make sure that your oats are finely ground in this recipe or use colloidal oatmeal in its place. Its purpose in this soap is to help soften the water and soothe itchy, inflamed skin. Lavender essential oil adds a lovely, calming scent, but it's optional. This recipe makes a wonderfully effective unscented soap, too!

YIELD: 7 TO 8 BARS

1 tbsp (7 g) rolled oats

4.18 oz (112 g) sodium hydroxide (lye)

9 oz (269 g) water

17 oz (482 g) lavender-infused olive oil (see page 17 for how to infuse oils)

8 oz (227 g) coconut oil

3 oz (85 g) sweet almond oil

2 tbsp (30 ml) lavender essential oil (optional)

Using an electric coffee grinder, grind the oats until they're finely powdered. Set aside, to add later in the recipe.

Wearing protective gloves and eyewear, carefully stir the lye into the water until completely dissolved. Set the solution aside in a safe place and let cool for about 30 to 40 minutes. The temperature should drop to around 100 to 110°F (38 to 43°C) during that time.

While the lye cools, weigh out the oils and gently heat them to a temperature of around 90 to 100°F (32 to 38°C). Pour the warmed oils into your soap-making pot or bowl, then add the cooled lye solution.

Hand stir with an immersion blender (powered off) for about 30 seconds, then turn the immersion blender on and mix the soap batter, alternating every 30 seconds or so with hand stirring to prevent the immersion blender's motor from burning out. Continue mixing until trace is reached. This can take anywhere from 2 to 10 minutes to reach trace. "Trace" means that the soap batter is thick enough to leave a faint, fleeting imprint when it's drizzled across itself.

(continued)

Lavender Oatmeal Soap (continued)

FOR COLD PROCESS SOAP

Stir in the ground oatmeal and lavender essential oil, if using. Pour the soap batter into a prepared soap mold, covering with a sheet of wax paper and then the mold's lid or a piece of cardboard. Tuck a towel or quilt around the mold to help hold the heat in. Let the soap stay in the mold for 24 to 48 hours, then remove and slice into bars. Allow the bars to cure in the open air for at least four weeks before using.

FOR HOT PROCESS SOAP

Pour the soap batter into a slow cooker turned on low heat. Cover with the lid and let cook for 1 hour, checking and stirring every 15 minutes. After the hour has passed, stir in the ground oatmeal and lavender essential oil, mixed with 1 tablespoon (15 ml) of water if your soap is very thick. Stir well and then spoon the cooked soap into a prepared mold. Allow it to firm up overnight, then remove from the mold and slice into bars. You can use the hot process soap right away, though it makes a longer-lasting bar if it cures in the open air for a few weeks.

Old-Fashioned Rose Soap

This lovely soap features real roses, creamy shea butter and nourishing rosehip seed oil. Rose petal-infused olive oil softens and conditions skin, while coconut oil adds plenty of bubbles and creates a harder bar of soap. Shea butter is not only great for your skin, but it adds additional hardness to the bar. Rosehip seed oil was included for its fantastic skin-regenerating and healing properties. Rose kaolin clay contributes a natural pink color, but you can use half as much for a paler shade of pink or leave it out completely for a creamy white bar instead.

YIELD: 7 TO 8 BARS

1 handful fresh or dried rose petals

10 oz (283 g) water

4.14 oz (117 g) sodium hydroxide (lye)

15 oz (425 g) rose petal-infused olive oil (see page 17 for how to infuse oils)

1 oz (28 g) rosehip seed oil

8 oz (227 g) coconut oil

4 oz (113 g) shea butter

2 oz (57 g) castor oil

2 tsp rose kaolin clay (optional, for color)

1 tbsp (15 ml) water

1 to 2 tbsp (15 to 30 ml) rose absolute or geranium essential oil (optional)

FOR THE ROSE-INFUSED WATER

Place the rose petals in a heatproof jar or container. Heat the water to a simmer and pour over the petals. Allow the rose infusion to steep until it's room temperature or cooler. Make sure that your tea is fairly light, and not a dark brown color, or it may affect the color of the finished soap. Strain the rose-infused water into a heavy-duty plastic or stainless steel bowl or pitcher.

FOR THE SOAP

Wearing gloves, goggles and long sleeves, pour the lye into the cooled rose petal infusion and carefully stir until it's fully dissolved. It may turn a dark brown color as it meets the lye, but that's okay at this point. Set the lye solution aside for 45 minutes to 1 hour or until cooled to approximately 100 to 110°F (38 to 43°C).

While the lye solution cools, weigh the olive, castor and rosehip seed oil and place in your soap mixing pot or container. In a double boiler, heat the coconut oil and shea butter until melted. Pour them into the container with the olive and castor oil. This should bring the temperature to somewhere around 90 to 100°F (32 to 38°C).

In a small bowl, stir together the rose kaolin clay, 1 tablespoon (15 ml) water and essential oil until smooth. This will be added at trace (for cold process soap) or after cook time (for hot process soap).

Combine the lye solution and the oils. Hand stir with an immersion blender (powered off) for about 30 seconds, then turn the immersion blender on and mix the soap batter, alternating every 30 seconds or so with hand stirring to prevent the immersion blender's motor from burning out. Continue mixing until trace is reached. This recipe will reach trace within a few minutes. "Trace" means that the soap batter is thick enough to leave a faint, fleeting imprint when it's drizzled across itself.

(continued)

Old-Fashioned Rose Soap (continued)

FOR COLD PROCESS SOAP

Thoroughly stir the clay, water and essential oil mixture into the soap. Pour the soap batter into a prepared soap mold, cover with a sheet of wax paper and then the mold's lid or a piece of cardboard. Tuck a towel or quilt around the mold to help hold the heat in. Let the soap stay in the mold for 24 to 48 hours, then remove and slice into bars. Allow the bars to cure in the open air for at least four weeks before using.

FOR HOT PROCESS SOAP

Pour the soap batter into a slow cooker turned on low heat. Cover with the lid and let cook for 1 hour, checking and stirring every 15 minutes. After the hour has passed, stir in the clay, water and essential oil mixture, then spoon the cooked soap into a prepared mold. Allow it to firm up overnight, then remove from the mold and slice into bars. You can use hot process soap right away, though it makes a longer-lasting bar if it cures in the open air for a few weeks.

Thyme & Witch Hazel Clear Skin Facial Bar

The skin-healing properties of raw honey, tamanu oil and antiseptic thyme combine with the astringency of witch hazel in this acne-fighting soap. Skin-softening olive oil and bubble-boosting coconut oil form the base of the recipe, while sunflower oil adds a silky lather and is great for all complexions. Castor oil promotes a better lathering experience, but if you don't have any on hand, you can substitute more olive oil instead. Tamanu oil packs a powerful punch, so only a small amount is needed for its powerful antimicrobial, anti-inflammatory and remarkable skin-regenerating benefits. Be aware that the addition of witch hazel to this soap tends to give it a slight medicinal smell. If you want to omit the witch hazel, you can do so; just increase the initial water amount by 1 ounce (28 g).

YIELD: 7 TO 8 BARS

½ cup (7 g) chopped fresh or dried thyme

8 oz (227 g) simmering hot water

4.17 oz (118 g) sodium hydroxide (lye)

½ oz (14 g) raw honey

1 oz (28 g) witch hazel

15 oz (425 g) olive oil

8 oz (227g) coconut oil

4 oz (113 g) sunflower oil

2 oz (57 g) castor oil

1 oz (28 g) tamanu oil

FOR THE THYME-INFUSED WATER
Place the thyme in a heatproof jar or pitcher. Pour the simmering hot water into the jar and let it steep for up to 1 hour, or until cool. Strain.

FOR THE SOAP
Pour the completely cooled tea into a heatproof plastic or stainless steel container. Wearing gloves, goggles and long sleeves, pour the lye into the cooled thyme-infused water and carefully stir until it's fully dissolved. It may turn a different color as it meets the lye, but that's okay at this point. Set the lye solution aside for 45 minutes to 1 hour or until cooled to approximately 100 to 110°F (38 to 43°C).

While the lye solution is cooling, blend the honey and witch hazel together in a small bowl and set aside. This will be added to the soap later, at trace (for cold process soap) or after cook time (for hot process soap).

Weigh out and gently heat the oils until they're about 90 to 100°F (32 to 38°C).

Pour the cooled lye solution into the oils. Hand stir with an immersion blender (powered off) for about 30 seconds, then turn the immersion blender on and mix the soap batter, alternating every 30 seconds or so with hand stirring to prevent the immersion blender's motor from burning out. Continue mixing until trace is reached. This recipe will usually reach trace within 3 to 5 minutes. "Trace" means that the soap batter is thick enough to leave a faint, fleeting imprint when it's drizzled across itself.

(continued)

Thyme & Witch Hazel
Clear Skin Facial Bar (continued)

FOR COLD PROCESS SOAP

Thoroughly stir the honey and witch hazel mixture into the soap, then pour the soap batter into a prepared soap mold. Honey tends to make soap heat up more than normal, so we don't need to cover or insulate this soap. Let the soap stay in the mold for 24 to 48 hours, then remove and slice into bars. Allow the bars to cure in the open air for at least four weeks before using.

FOR HOT PROCESS SOAP

Pour the soap batter into a slow cooker turned on low heat. Cover with the lid and let cook for 1 hour, checking and stirring every 15 minutes. After the hour has passed, stir in the witch hazel and honey, then spoon the cooked soap into a prepared mold. Allow it to firm up overnight, then remove from the mold and slice into bars. You can use the hot process soap right away, though it makes a longer-lasting bar if it cures in the open air for a few weeks.

For best results, use this soap to wash your face nightly, followed by an antiacne toner such as Dandelion Thyme Vinegar Toner & Tonic (page 45). If needed, apply a light moisturizer such as Grapeseed & Thyme Lotion for oily skin (page 85).

Sunflower Shampoo Bar

Shampoo bars are a popular and eco-friendly way to wash hair. They work for many hair types, but if you have hard water, you may find it difficult to completely rinse the suds out. Be sure to follow a shampoo bar wash with a vinegar hair rinse to soften your locks and prevent buildup. Sunflower petals and oil make a great addition to shampoo bars since the extract is used in some high-end products to condition hair and add shine. Argan oil is included because of its abilities to nourish, strengthen and protect hair, but if it's out of your budget, you can use sweet almond oil or more shea butter instead. Olive oil nourishes and conditions, while coconut oil hardens soap and adds plenty of bubbles. Shea butter moisturizes hair and scalp and also helps harden the bar. Small amounts of castor oil are often added to soap recipes to help stabilize lather, but in the case of shampoo bars, a higher amount is used and is almost essential for a great shampooing experience.

YIELD: 7 TO 8 BARS

4.02 oz (114 g) sodium hyrdoxide (lye)

10 oz (283 g) water

8 oz (227 g) coconut oil

2 oz (57 g) shea butter

10 oz (283 g) sunflower-infused olive oil (see page 17 for how to infuse oils)

4 oz (113 g) castor oil

4 oz (113 g) sunflower oil

1 oz (28 g) argan oil

2 tbsp (30 ml) lemongrass essential oil (optional)

Wearing protective gloves and eyewear, carefully stir the lye into the water until completely dissolved. Set the solution aside in a safe place and let cool for about 30 to 40 minutes. The temperature should drop to around 100 to 110°F (38 to 43°C) during that time.

While the lye cools, weigh out the oils and gently heat them to a temperature of around 90 to 100°F (32 to 38°C). Pour the warmed oils into your soap-making pot or bowl, then add the cooled lye solution.

Hand stir with an immersion blender (powered off) for about 30 seconds, then turn the immersion blender on and mix the soap batter, alternating every 30 seconds or so with hand stirring to prevent the immersion blender's motor from burning out. Continue mixing until trace is reached. This can take anywhere from 2 to 10 minutes to reach trace. "Trace" means that the soap batter is thick enough to leave a faint, fleeting imprint when it's drizzled across itself.

(continued)

Sunflower Shampoo Bar (continued)

FOR COLD PROCESS SOAP

Stir in the essential oil, if using, then pour the soap into a prepared mold. Let it stay in the mold for 24 to 48 hours, then remove and slice into bars. Let the bars cure in the open air for at least four weeks before using.

FOR HOT PROCESS SOAP

Pour the soap batter into a slow cooker turned on low heat. Cover with the lid and let cook for 1 hour, checking and stirring every 15 minutes. After the hour has passed, stir in the lemongrass essential oil, if using, then spoon the cooked soap into a prepared mold. Allow it to firm up overnight, then remove from the mold and slice into bars. You can use the hot process soap right away, though it makes a longer-lasting bar if it cures in the open air for a few weeks.

To use the shampoo bar, just wet your hair with water and then gently rub the bar over it, massaging the lather onto your scalp and to the ends of your hair with your fingers. For long hair, you may want to work up a lather with your hands first and then rub it through your hair, to avoid tangles. Rinse well, then follow with a diluted vinegar rinse for a clean and healthy shine!

Hollyhock Shampoo Bar

This bar features moisturizing hollyhock leaves and flowers, making it ideal for normal to dry hair. Olive oil softens and conditions hair and scalp, while coconut oil adds lots of bubbles and hardness to soap recipes. Sweet almond oil and shea butter help to moisturize and relieve a dry, itchy scalp. A generous amount of castor oil ensures lots of lather and a great shampooing experience. I like to add a blend of lavender and litsea cubeba essential oils for a fresh floral scent, but you can leave them out for an unscented version. Be sure to follow a wash with a shampoo bar with a diluted vinegar hair rinse to help restore pH and promote shine.

YIELD: 7 TO 8 BARS

4.09 oz (116 g) sodium hydroxide (lye)

10 oz (283 g) water

10 oz (283 g) hollyhock-infused olive oil (see page 17 for how to infuse oils)

8 oz (227 g) coconut oil

4 oz (113 g) sweet almond oil

4 oz (113 g) castor oil

2 oz (57 g) shea butter

1 tbsp (15 ml) lavender essential oil (optional)

½ tbsp (7.5 ml) litsea cubeba essential oil (optional)

Wearing protective gloves and eyewear, carefully stir the lye into the water in a heatproof plastic or stainless steel container until completely dissolved. Set the solution aside in a safe place and let cool for about 30 to 40 minutes. The temperature should drop to around 100 to 110°F (38 to 43°C) during that time.

While the lye solution cools, weigh out the oils and butter and gently heat them to a temperature of around 90 to 100°F (32 to 38°C). Pour the warmed oils into your soap-making pot or bowl, then add the cooled lye solution.

Hand stir with an immersion blender (powered off) for about 30 seconds, then turn the immersion blender on and mix the soap batter, alternating every 30 seconds or so with hand stirring to prevent the immersion blender's motor from burning out. Continue mixing until trace is reached. This can take anywhere from 2 to 10 minutes. "Trace" means that the soap batter is thick enough to leave a faint, fleeting imprint when it's drizzled across itself.

(continued)

FOR COLD PROCESS SOAP

Stir in the essential oil, if using, then pour the soap into a prepared mold. Let it stay in the mold for 24 to 48 hours, then remove and slice into bars. Let the bars cure in the open air for at least four weeks before using.

FOR HOT PROCESS SOAP

Pour the soap batter into a slow cooker turned on low heat. Cover with the lid and let cook for 1 hour, checking and stirring every 15 minutes. After the hour has passed, stir in the lavender and litsea cubeba essential oils, if using, then spoon the cooked soap into a prepared mold. Allow it to firm up overnight, then remove from the mold and slice into bars. You can use the hot process soap right away, though it makes a longer-lasting bar if it cures in the open air for a few weeks.

To use a shampoo bar, just wet your hair with water and then gently rub the bar over it, massaging the lather onto your scalp and to the ends of your hair with your fingers. For long hair, you may want to work up a lather with your hands first and then rub it through your hair, to avoid tangles. Rinse well, follow with a diluted vinegar rinse and enjoy beautiful, shiny hair all day long!

Dandelion Scrub Bar

A scattering of poppy seeds dots this brightly scented soap, giving texture and a gentle exfoliating effect. Dandelion flowers, which are wonderful for treating rough, dry skin, are infused into skin-softening olive oil, then combined with bubbly coconut and nourishing sunflower oil. This bar is perfect for scrubbing away dirt and grime from hands, making it a wonderful gift for the gardener or farmer in your life! It can also be used as an all-over body bar.

YIELD: 7 TO 8 BARS

4.19 oz (119 oz) sodium hydroxide (lye)

8.5 oz (241 g) water

6 oz (454 g) dandelion-infused olive oil (see page 17 for how to infuse oil)

3 oz (85 g) sunflower oil

8 oz (227 g) coconut oil

3 oz (85 g) cocoa butter

2 tbsp (30 ml) lemongrass essential oil

½ tbsp (5 g) poppy seeds

For smoother, cleaner skin, use daily and follow with a light but effective moisturizer, such as Basic Calendula Lotion (page 81).

Wearing protective gloves and eyewear, carefully stir the lye into the water in a heatproof plastic or stainless steel container until completely dissolved. Set the mixture aside for 30 to 40 minutes, or until the temperature is around 100 to 110°F (38 to 43°C).

While the lye solution cools, weigh out the dandelion-infused olive oil and sunflower oil and pour them into your soap-making pot or bowl. In a double boiler, heat the coconut oil and cocoa butter on low until completely melted. Pour the melted butter combination into the other oils and check the temperature. If needed, heat the oils to around 90 to 100°F (32 to 38°C).

Pour the lye solution into the warmed oils. Hand stir with an immersion blender (powered off) for about 30 seconds, then turn the immersion blender on and mix the soap batter, alternating every 30 seconds or so with hand stirring to prevent the immersion blender's motor from burning out. Continue mixing until trace is reached. This can take anywhere from 2 to 10 minutes. "Trace" means that the soap batter is thick enough to leave a faint, fleeting imprint when it's drizzled across itself.

FOR COLD PROCESS SOAP

Add the lemongrass essential oil and poppy seeds, then stir until they're fully incorporated. Pour the soap into a prepared mold. Let it stay in the mold for 24 to 48 hours, then remove and slice into bars. Let the bars cure in the open air for at least 4 weeks before using.

FOR HOT PROCESS SOAP

Pour the soap batter into a slow cooker turned on low heat. Cover with the lid and let cook for 1 hour, checking and stirring every 15 minutes. After the hour has passed, stir in the poppy seeds and lemongrass essential oil, then spoon the cooked soap into a prepared mold. Allow it to firm up overnight, then remove from the mold and slice into bars. You can use the hot process soap right away, though it makes a longer-lasting bar if it cures in the open air for a few weeks.

Carrot & Calendula Soap

This delightful soap is a treat for all skin types. Carrots are a nutritional powerhouse full of antioxidants and vitamin A, while calendula-infused olive oil soothes and softens skin. Coconut oil helps make soap bubbly and hard, while sunflower oil nourishes all skin types. Castor oil is a great addition to soap since it helps boost and stabilize lather. Raw honey adds a little something extra special to the bar, but if you're vegan, it can be omitted. Carrot soap is popular for use as a facial bar, but can also be used to wash your body for softer, smoother skin.

YIELD: 7 TO 8 BARS

6 oz (198 g) bottled or home-pressed 100% carrot juice

3 oz (57 g) water

4.22 oz (120 g) sodium hydroxide (lye)

15 oz (425 g) calendula-infused olive oil (see page 17 for how to infuse oil)

8 oz (227 g) coconut oil

4.5 oz (128 g) sunflower oil

2.5 oz (71 g) castor oil

1 tbsp (21 g) raw honey (optional)

1 tbsp (15 ml) water, for hot process version

Place the carrot juice and water in a heatproof plastic or stainless steel pitcher. Wearing protective gloves and eyewear, slowly stir the lye into the diluted juice until fully dissolved. The mixture will probably be a bright shade of orange and may smell unpleasant during this phase—this is normal. Set the mixture aside for 30 to 40 minutes, or until the temperature is around 100 to 110°F (38 to 43°C).

While the lye solution cools, weigh out the oils and pour them into your soap-making pot or bowl. Gently heat them to around 90 to 100°F (32 to 38°C).

Pour the lye and carrot juice solution into the warm oils. Hand stir with an immersion blender (powered off) for about 30 seconds, then turn the immersion blender on and mix the soap batter, alternating every 30 seconds or so with hand stirring to prevent the immersion blender's motor from burning out. Continue mixing until trace is reached. This can take anywhere from 2 to 10 minutes. "Trace" means that the soap batter is thick enough to leave a faint, fleeting imprint when it's drizzled across itself.

FOR COLD PROCESS SOAP

Add the honey, if using, and stir one more time until it's fully incorporated. The soap will still be a dark or medium orange at this point, but will lighten as it cures. Pour the soap into a prepared mold. Since it has honey and juice in it, it may tend to heat up faster than other soaps, so you don't need to cover the mold. If you see a crack developing in the top, it means the soap is getting too hot. Move it to a cooler room or even your refrigerator for 2 to 3 hours to cool it down. Let it stay in the mold for 2 to 3 days, then remove and slice into bars. Let the bars cure in the open air for around 4 weeks before using.

FOR HOT PROCESS SOAP

Pour the soap batter into a slow cooker turned on low heat. Cover with the lid and let cook for 1 hour, checking and stirring every 15 minutes. Stir the honey and water together until completely blended. The extra water will help the honey stir into the hot soap, with a reduced chance of scorching. After the hour has passed, stir in the diluted honey, then spoon the cooked soap into a prepared mold. Allow it to firm up overnight, then remove from the mold and slice into bars. You can use the hot process soap right away, though it makes a longer-lasting bar if it cures in the open air for a few weeks.

Cucumber Mint Soap

Cool and creamy, this soap is a refreshing treat on a hot summer day. The French green clay not only gives each bar a pretty color, but also helps soothe itchy skin caused by bug bites or heat rash. Mint-infused olive oil conditions skin, while coconut and castor oil add a bubbly lather. Extra nourishing avocado oil is loaded with essential fatty acids to help promote beautiful skin. Perky peppermint, with its cooling, anti-inflammatory properties, makes the perfect companion for cucumber, an astringent skin toner in its own right. The essential oil also adds a wonderful scent and feel, making bath time with this soap an energizing and uplifting experience!

YIELD: 7 TO 8 BARS

1/4 of a fresh, unpeeled cucumber (approximately 2 to 3 oz [55 to 85 g])

8 to 9 oz (227 to 255 g) cold water

4.17 oz (118 g) sodium hydroxide (lye)

17 oz (482 g) mint-infused olive oil (see page 17 for how to infuse oil)

8 oz (227 g) coconut oil

3 oz (85 g) avocado oil

2 oz (57 g) castor oil

2 tbsp peppermint essential oil

1/2 tbsp (8 g) French green clay

1 tbsp (15 ml) water

Purée the cucumber and about 4 ounces (120 ml) of water together in a food processor or blender. Strain the resulting liquid with a fine mesh sieve or strainer so there are no pieces of cucumber left; you'll only need the juice from it. Add additional cold water, as needed, until you have 9 ounces (255 g) of cucumber and water slurry.

Place the mixture in a heatproof plastic or stainless steel pitcher. Wearing protective gloves and eyewear, slowly stir the lye into the cucumber water until it's fully dissolved. Set the mixture aside for 30 to 40 minutes, or until the temperature is around 100 to 110°F (38 to 43°C).

While the lye solution cools, weigh out the oils and pour into your soap-making pot or bowl. Gently heat them to around 90 to 100°F (32 to 38°C).

In a small bowl, stir together the essential oil, clay and water to make a thick paste that will be added later in the recipe.

Pour the lye and cucumber water solution into the warm oils. Hand stir with an immersion blender (powered off) for about 30 seconds, then turn the immersion blender on and mix the soap batter, alternating every 30 seconds or so with hand stirring to prevent the immersion blender's motor from burning out. Continue mixing until trace is reached. This can take anywhere from 2 to 10 minutes. "Trace" means that the soap batter is thick enough to leave a faint, fleeting imprint when drizzled across itself.

FOR COLD PROCESS SOAP

Add the combined essential oil, clay and water, then stir one more time until they're fully incorporated. Pour the soap into a prepared soap mold. Cover with a sheet of wax paper and then the mold top, if it has one, or a piece of cardboard. Tuck a towel or blanket around the mold, to help keep the heat in. Let the soap stay in the mold for 24 to 48 hours then unmold and turn the soap loaf out on a sheet of wax paper. Cut the soap into bars and cure in the open air for around 4 weeks before using.

FOR HOT PROCESS SOAP

Pour the soap batter into a slow cooker turned on low heat. Cover with the lid and let cook for 1 hour, checking and stirring every 15 minutes. After the hour has passed, stir in the combined essential oil, clay and water, then spoon the cooked soap into a prepared mold. Allow it to firm up overnight, then remove from the mold and slice into bars. You can use the hot process soap right away, though it makes a longer-lasting bar if it cures in the open air for a few weeks.

➣ See picture on page 152.

Coconut Laundry Soap & Stain Stick

This pure coconut oil soap is intended for laundry purposes only. It has no extra oils or fats in it, making it better suited for cleaning tough stains on clothes rather than your skin. It can be used as a stain stick, as detailed below, or to turn it into a homemade Lavender Laundry Detergent recipe, see page 226. I often leave laundry soap plain, but you can add essential oils for natural fragrance if you'd like. Lavender, peppermint or lemongrass are three fresh, clean scents you may want to consider. Since pure coconut oil sets up so quickly and can be employed for laundry use after only two weeks of cure time, I prefer to make this soap using the cold process method only.

YIELD: 7 TO 8 BARS

10 oz (283 g) water

5.15 oz (146 g) sodium hydroxide (lye)

28 oz (794 g) coconut oil

2 tbsp (30 ml) essential oil, for scent (optional)

Place the water in a heatproof plastic or stainless steel pitcher. Wearing protective gloves and eyewear, slowly stir the lye into the water until fully dissolved. Set the mixture aside for 30 to 40 minutes, or until the temperature is around 100 to 110°F (38 to 43°C).

While the lye solution cools, warm the coconut oil until it's melted and around 90 to 100°F (32 to 38°C). Pour it into your soap-making pot or bowl.

Pour the lye solution into the warm coconut oil and stir by hand for 1 to 2 minutes. Most often, coconut oil soap will set up quickly and you may not need to use your immersion blender. If it doesn't start to thicken after that amount of time, use your immersion blender in intermittent bursts for another 1 to 2 minutes, or until trace is reached.

Pour the soap into a prepared mold. Leave the mold uncovered and let it sit undisturbed for 2 to 3 hours. You want to cut coconut oil soap much sooner than other types of soap, since it hardens quickly and will be crumbly and difficult to cut if you wait too long. After 2 hours, check to see if the soap is firm enough to slice into bars. Even though it becomes solid sooner than other soaps, it may still be caustic for another 12 to 24 hours, so make sure you're wearing your gloves for this step.

Set the bars on sheets of wax paper or coated cooling racks and allow to cure in the open air for around 2 weeks before using.

To use as a stain stick, cut each bar of soap into halves or thirds to make easy-to-hold stick-shaped pieces. Wet the soiled area with plain water and rub the soap directly into it until a lather forms. Launder as usual. These stain sticks should work on most types of machine-washable clothing, but always test a small spot out first, to be sure.

Herbal Home Remedies

This is the chapter where your flowers and herbs can really shine!

Here, you'll learn how to make remedies and potions for treating pains, coughs, sore throats and other such maladies. I share several of the time-tested recipes that I use to keep my family healthy and well.

It's a joy to spend time outdoors when the weather is warm and sunny, but bee stings and bug bites can put a real damper on the fun. Try whipping up a batch of Bug Bite Powder (page 197) or portable Lavender Bug Bite Sticks (page 192) for a dose of quick relief. To help keep bugs away in the first place, try mixing together some Catnip & Basil Insect Repellant Spray (page 191).

Working and playing outdoors all day can leave you with sore muscles in need of serious relief. Dandelion oil is fantastic and just what you need to ease away aches and pains. You can use it to make a handy roll-on Lavender Dandelion Pain Relief Oil (page 198) or a quick-acting Dandelion Magnesium Lotion (page 206), which has helped many friends and family members who suffer from nighttime leg cramps.

When fall and winter roll around, colds and flu aren't far behind. Keep a stash of remedies on hand, such as Oregano Oxymel (page 202) or Violet Flower Sore Throat Syrup (page 205), to help speed up recovery time and help your loved ones feel better fast!

Catnip & Basil Insect Repellant Spray

This homemade bug spray features catnip, for its reported ability to repel mosquitoes just as well as DEET, and basil, which contains compounds that repel flies, mosquitoes and other pesky critters. To make this spray most effective, be sure to add at least one of the essential oils listed. According to current aromatherapy guidelines, basil, citronella and lemongrass essential oils should not be used on children under the age of 2 and eucalyptus should be reserved for those who are age 10 or over.

YIELD: 1 CUP (250 ML)

½ cup (10 g) fresh catnip and basil leaves, chopped

1 cup (250 ml) witch hazel

Citronella, basil, lemongrass and/or lemon eucalyptus essential oils

Water, for diluting

FOR THE HERB-INFUSED WITCH HAZEL

Place the catnip and basil leaves in a pint (500-ml) jar. Pour the witch hazel over the herbs. You may need to add a little extra witch hazel to ensure that the herbs are completely covered. Cap the jar and tuck it away in a dark cabinet for 1 week, then remove and strain. The finished infused witch hazel should stay fresh at least 9 months to 1 year.

FOR THE BUG SPRAY

Fill a small 2-ounce (60-ml) glass spray bottle a little over halfway with the infused witch hazel. Add 3 or 4 drops total of your favorite bug-repelling essential oils, such as citronella, basil, lemongrass or lemon. Fill the rest of the bottle with plain water, cap and shake.

Shake frequently before and during use, to make sure the essential oils stay dispersed throughout the spray. Spritz lightly on your arms, legs and other areas you'd like to keep bug free. If gnats are a problem while you work outdoors, spritz the brim and inside of your hat to keep them away. If you're pregnant, nursing or have other health concerns, check with a doctor before using the listed essential oils.

Depending on your body chemistry and the level of bugs in the area, this spray should help for anywhere from 30 minutes to 2 hours. Reapply as needed.

Variation: Lemon balm, lavender and mint are other effective, natural bug-repelling herbs that can be substituted for catnip or basil, if needed.

Lavender Bug Bite Sticks

These all-natural bug bite sticks are perfect for outdoor enthusiasts on the go. Lavender is a well-loved and gentle herb that helps soothe the itchiness and discomfort that minor bug bites can bring. As a bonus, it also acts as a mild insect repellant, helping to reduce the chance of new bites. I like to use sunflower oil in this recipe, since it's suitable for all skin types and has been shown to be an effective healer of broken or damaged skin, but you can use another light oil, such as olive or sweet almond, instead.

YIELD: 7 TO 8 (0.15 OZ) TUBES

½ cup (125 ml) sunflower oil

¼ cup (9 g) dried lavender flowers

1 tbsp (9 g) tightly packed beeswax, grated or pastilles

Few drops of lavender essential oil

Infuse the sunflower oil with lavender flowers, using one of the methods on page 17. Strain.

In a heatproof jar or container, combine 3 tablespoons (45 ml) of lavender-infused oil with the beeswax. Set the jar down into a saucepan containing 1 to 2 inches (2.5 to 5 cm) of water, forming a makeshift double boiler. Place the pan over a medium-low burner until the wax is melted. Stir in the lavender essential oil, then pour into lip balm tubes.

Depending on the weather and how you measured your beeswax, you may find that the consistency is too soft or too firm. If that happens, just melt the ingredients again and add more beeswax (for a firmer product) or oil (for a softer one).

Dab on bee stings, bug bites and other itchy spots as needed.

Calamine Rose Lotion

The sight of calamine lotion reminds many people of childhood cases of the chicken pox, poison ivy rashes or other miserably itchy skin ailments! Make your own economical version of the effective classic, minus the extra additives. Rose petals are used in this recipe for their astringent and skin-soothing properties. If fresh roses aren't on hand, try using half as many dried petals instead. Witch hazel cools and reduces inflammation, baking soda eases itching and white kaolin clay binds up irritants while helping to soothe skin. Rose kaolin clay essentially works in the same way as the white version and can be added to this recipe in order to obtain the classic pink color of traditional calamine.

YIELD: 4 OUNCES (125 ML)

½ cup (5 g) fresh rose petals

1 cup (250 ml) witch hazel

¼ cup (24 g) white kaolin clay

1 tbsp (6 g) rose kaolin clay
(optional, for color)

¼ cup (62 g) baking soda

FOR THE ROSE-INFUSED WITCH HAZEL

Place the rose petals in a pint (500-ml) jar and cover with the witch hazel. Cap and tuck away in a dark cabinet for around 1 week. If using pink or red roses, the witch hazel should take on a shade of the same color. Strain. The finished witch hazel should stay fresh for 6 to 9 months, when stored in a cool, dark location, though the color will fade over time.

Reserve ¼ cup (60 ml) for this recipe.

FOR THE CALAMINE ROSE LOTION

Combine the white kaolin clay, rose kaolin clay (if using) and baking soda in a half-pint (250 ml) canning jar. Pour the reserved rose-infused witch hazel into the jar. Stir well. Avoid shaking the jar, since the liquid will splash up on the sides and it will dry out more easily. While calamine has the word "lotion" in its name, it's not actually lotion-like. The texture is more like a thick chalky liquid.

Seal tightly and store in a cool place. Because it contains witch hazel instead of water, your calamine lotion should remain fresh for at least 1 or 2 months. If it starts to dry out, simply stir in more witch hazel.

To use, dip a cotton ball or swab into the lotion and dab on itchy spots, rashes and other skin irritations. Allow the calamine lotion to dry on your skin.

→ See photo on page 188.

Lemongrass Cream Deodorant

This wonderful deodorant recipe was developed and shared with me by my friend Kay, who graciously agreed to let me share it with you. I did a tiny bit of tweaking and added some germ-busting lemongrass to the mix, but you could also use lavender or mint. I've tried a lot of homemade deodorants, but this is my favorite by far! You only need to rub a tiny dab under each arm for it to be effective.

YIELD: 4 OUNCES (125 ML)

2 tbsp (1 g) dried lemongrass, crumbled

1½ oz (43 g) sunflower oil

1 oz (28 g) beeswax

1 oz (28 g) shea butter

¼ cup (54 g) coconut oil

1 tbsp (14 g) baking soda

1 tbsp (14 g) arrowroot powder

¼ tsp lemongrass essential oil

Infuse the lemongrass and sunflower oil, using one of the methods on page 17. Strain and reserve 1 teaspoon of infused oil for this recipe.

Place the beeswax, shea butter and coconut oil in a heatproof jar. Set the jar down into a saucepan containing 1 to 2 inches (2.5 to 5 cm) of water and heat over a medium-low burner until the wax is melted. Remove from heat.

Stir in the baking soda, arrowroot and lemongrass essential oil. Stir frequently over the next 5 to 10 minutes as the mixture cools. It will turn thick and creamy. Spoon the finished deodorant into a jar. The texture will stay soft and spreadable, so it won't be quite firm enough to pour in a traditional deodorant container.

To use, scoop a small amount (about ¹⁄₁₆ teaspoon) out of the jar, using the tip of your finger, and gently rub it into your underarm area. Repeat the process under your other arm. Depending on body chemistry and environment, you may find that you only need to apply this once daily, though very hot weather sometimes requires a second application, later in the day.

Shelf life is around 9 to 12 months as long as water is not introduced to the jar.

Bug Bite Powder

This is a favorite home remedy that my kids use all the time. I made it to mimic an expensive product that I had bought in the past and loved, until I realized that it was not much more than kaolin clay that could easily be bought for just a few dollars per pound. I combine the clay with finely ground calendula, an herb useful for taming inflamed and irritated skin, to create a powder that's perfect for dabbing on bug bites, bee stings, acne and other minor skin irritations. It's a bit messier to apply than the Lavender Bug Bite Sticks (page 192), but makes up for it in effectiveness!

YIELD: 1 1/2 TABLESPOONS (6 G)

1/4 cup (1 g) dried calendula flowers and petals

1 tbsp (5 g) kaolin clay

Grind the calendula flowers in an electric coffee grinder or mortar and pestle. Rub the resulting powder through a fine mesh sieve. Return the larger pieces to the coffee grinder once more, then rub through the sieve again. This should result in an extremely fine, silky powder.

Mix with the kaolin clay and store in a glass jar. Kaolin clay has a long shelf life, but because of the dried calendula portion, this powder will be at its best if used up within 1 year.

To use, dab on bug bites or other skin irritations. One application may be all you need, but if the itching or discomfort returns, apply again as needed. You can also mix a small pinch with a few drops of water or witch hazel to make a paste.

Lavender Dandelion Pain Relief Oil

A glass roll-on bottle makes it easy to apply this oil over achy joints, sore muscles and other areas in need of pain relief. Use a light oil that absorbs quickly into the skin for this recipe, such as sweet almond, grapeseed or apricot kernel oil. Tamanu oil is highly recommended for its anti-inflammatory properties, but if cost is an issue, it can be replaced with more sweet almond oil. Lavender calms and soothes sore muscles, while the mild analgesic properties of dandelion flowers offer relief from aches and pains.

YIELD: 4 OUNCES (120 ML) PAIN RELIEF OIL

½ cup (120 ml) sweet almond oil

¼ cup (9 g) dried lavender flowers

¼ cup (2 g) dried dandelion flowers

1 tbsp (15 ml) tamanu oil

2 to 3 drops lavender essential oil

Infuse the sweet almond oil with the dried lavender and dandelion flowers, using one of the methods on page 17.

Strain the finished oil, then add the tamanu oil and lavender essential oil.

Pour into glass roll-on bottles for easy application, or store in a small jar and use as a massage oil.

Variation: Other herbs that work well in a pain relief oil include arnica flowers, comfrey leaf, comfrey root and goldenrod. If warmth makes your aches and pains feel better, you can also try adding a pinch of dried ginger to the infusing oils.

Basil Mint Sore Throat Spray

Besides being a culinary superstar, basil has antibacterial, expectorant, sinus-opening and mild pain-relieving properties, making it a wonderful addition to this homemade sore throat spray. Here, it's paired with mint, for its refreshing taste and ability to cool and relieve inflammation. Raw honey is a powerful healer that helps coat and soothe painful throat tissue. The high concentration adds sweetness and helps preserve the herbal infusion longer than its normal shelf life of two days. For a mild throat-numbing effect and an extra boost against viruses, try adding echinacea or spilanthes tincture to your throat spray. The alcohol in the tincture will extend the shelf life by several additional weeks.

YIELD: 4 OUNCES (120 ML)

¼ cup (3 g) chopped fresh or frozen mint

2 to 3 leaves of fresh or frozen basil

¼ cup (60 ml) boiling water

3 tbsp (45 ml) raw honey

Few drops of peppermint extract, for flavor

1 tbsp (15 ml) echinacea or spilanthes tincture (optional)

Place the mint and basil leaves into a heatproof mug or jar and pour the boiling water over them. Cover and steep for 20 minutes, then strain. Stir in the raw honey and a few drops of peppermint extract, if desired. Add the tincture, if using, and mix well.

Pour into a small spray bottle. Store in the refrigerator and use within 1 week, unless you added a tincture, then it should last for 3 to 4 weeks, if refrigerated between uses.

To use, shake well and spritz the spray once or twice into your mouth, aiming toward the back of your throat, as often as needed. If your sore throat persists or you feel increasingly worse, consult your health care provider.

Variation: For an extra antiviral boost, try adding lemon balm to this recipe. If you suffer from swollen tonsils, calendula flower may help as well. Keep in mind that calendula should not be taken internally by those who are pregnant.

Oregano Oxymel

Oxymels are tangy sweet and sour herbal syrups that are a traditional remedy for treating coughs and sore throats. Oregano is an antimicrobial powerhouse that's able to knock out a wide variety of germs. Apple cider vinegar is used as a tonic to promote health, and raw honey contains compounds that fight infection. Consider the amounts of vinegar and honey given below to be a flexible starting point; the ratios can be adjusted to suit your taste. Since the shelf life of oxymels is fairly long, try making a batch during the summer, when oregano is in season, and tuck it away for use during winter's cold and flu season.

YIELD: ²/₃ CUP (160 ML)

⅓ cup (5 g) chopped fresh oregano leaves

⅓ cup (80 ml) apple cider vinegar

⅓ cup (80 ml) raw honey

Place the chopped oregano in a half-pint (250-ml) canning jar. Pour the vinegar over the leaves and stir. Next, pour the honey into the jar and stir again. If you'd like a sweeter syrup, try using more honey than vinegar. If you prefer tangy, use more vinegar. Both honey and vinegar act as preservatives here, so you can't mess up this recipe by altering the amounts of either one.

Cap the jar with a nonmetallic lid and shake well. If you don't have a nonmetallic lid, place a sheet of wax paper or plastic wrap between the jar and lid, to prevent corrosion from the vinegar.

Set the oxymel aside for 2 to 3 weeks, to allow the flavors to meld and the benefits of oregano to infuse into the vinegar and honey. Strain and store in a cool, dark place. Shelf life is at least 1 year.

Take oxymels by the spoonful several times a day, or as needed, for sore throat, congested cough and the general discomforts of colds and flu. If your symptoms worsen or you have concerns, contact your health care provider.

Tip: Fresh oregano is ideal, but you can use dried if it's not available.

Variation: No oregano? Try basil or thyme instead.

Violet Flower Sore Throat Syrup

This tasty syrup gently helps to relieve the bothersome discomfort caused by the cough and sore throat that accompany minor colds. Violets are soothing, cooling and high in vitamin C, while raw honey is a natural antimicrobial that coats inflamed tissues.

YIELD: 1 CUP (240 ML)

½ cup (10 g) fresh or frozen violet flowers

½ cup (120 ml) boiling water

½ cup (120 ml) raw honey

Place the violet flowers in a heatproof pitcher or canning jar and pour the boiling water over them.

Allow the flowers to steep for around 1 hour, or until room temperature, then strain. At this point, the infusion should be a dark blue color. You can make your violet syrup right away or place the violet infusion in the refrigerator overnight. The flower infusion can also be frozen for 6 to 9 months, if you'd like to make some at a later time.

When ready to make your syrup, place the violet flower infusion in a small saucepan and gently heat until warm. Try to keep the temperature under 110°F (43°C) in order to preserve all of the benefits of raw honey.

Remove the pan from the heat and stir in the honey until completely incorporated. Pour into a glass bottle or jar with a tight-fitting lid.

To use, take 1 to 3 teaspoons (5 to 15 ml) of syrup every 3 or 4 hours, as needed, for minor coughs and sore throats, keeping in mind that violet is also a mild laxative. Store the sore throat syrup in the refrigerator and use within 1 month. You can also freeze individual doses in ice cube trays to extend the shelf life for use throughout the year. Simply thaw at room temperature and take the syrup as usual.

If your symptoms persist or worsen, check with a qualified health care provider.

Tip: Honey and honey-containing products should not be given to children under the age of 1 year old.

Dandelion Magnesium Lotion

Experts posit that much of the population does not get enough magnesium in their daily diet. This can lead to headaches, leg cramps and a host of other subtle ailments. Beside baths with magnesium sulfate (Epsom salts) and magnesium supplements, another way to get more of this vital mineral is through the application of magnesium oil to the skin. Because the straight oil can be drying and irritating for some, it works well to couch it in a lotion or cream, especially ones containing soothing aloe. Dandelions were chosen for this recipe because the flowers have mild analgesic (pain-relieving) properties, making this cream especially helpful for leg cramps and other growing pains.

YIELD: 3.5 OUNCES (105 ML)

2 tbsp (30 ml) dandelion-infused oil (see page 17 for how to infuse oil)

3 tsp (6 g) emulsifying NF wax

2 tbsp (30 ml) magnesium oil

2 tbsp (30 ml) distilled water

1 tbsp (15 ml) aloe vera gel

2 to 3 drops lavender essential oil (optional)

Natural preservative (optional)

Add the dandelion-infused oil and emulsifying wax to a heatproof jar or upcycled tin can.

In spite of its name, magnesium oil is actually water based, so measure it out with the water and aloe and place in a half-pint (250-ml) canning jar.

Place both containers into a saucepan containing 1 to 2 inches (2.5 to 5 cm) of water, then set the pan over a medium-low burner. Keep both containers in the pan for around 10 minutes. This gives time for the wax to fully melt and the water, aloe and magnesium oil combination to reach a nearly matching temperature of around 150°F (66°C). Remove from heat.

Carefully pour the hot contents of the two containers into a heatproof mixing bowl or measuring pitcher. As they're poured together, the separate mixtures will begin to emulsify upon contact and turn a milky white color.

Using a fork or small whisk, stir the lotion briskly for 30 seconds, then set it aside to cool down for around 5 minutes. To speed up the cooling process, place your mixing container down into a bowl partially filled with ice cubes and water. Stir occasionally, for around 30 seconds at a time, as the lotion cools and thickens. Stir in the lavender essential oil, if using.

If you're adding a natural preservative, check the temperature and see if it's the proper time to do so. Recommended temperature will vary according to type, but preservatives are usually added when the lotion is cooling.

Pour or spoon the lotion into a bottle or jar. The lotion will continue to thicken as it sets up. Keep tops and lids off until it's completely cool, to prevent condensation from building up on the lid. If you didn't add a preservative, store your cream in the refrigerator and use within 2 weeks. Apply to legs, feet and back at night, or as needed when leg cramps strike.

Aloe Rose Sunburn & Hot Flash Spray

The calming, healing properties of rose shine in this fantastic spray that helps cool and ease the discomfort of sunburn and other flushed skin conditions. Witch hazel fights inflammation and heat, while aloe soothes and heals damaged skin. Apple cider vinegar is a traditional remedy for sunburn, so a small amount was added to this recipe. It doesn't really lend much smell, but if you're sensitive to the scent, use more witch hazel in its place. Storing the spray in the refrigerator adds an extra level of refreshing coolness and also helps extend the shelf life.

YIELD: 5 OUNCES (150 ML)

¼ cup (60 ml) witch hazel

¼ cup (60 ml) aloe vera gel

¼ cup (4 g) fresh rose petals

1 tbsp (15 ml) apple cider vinegar

1 tbsp (15 ml) water

Using a small food processor, blend all of the ingredients together until the mixture is light pink and frothy, with specks of rose petals visible. Strain.

Pour into a spray bottle and store in the refrigerator. Spritz on your neck, arms, legs and back as needed. You may also use this on your face; just make sure to close your eyes before spraying. If the spray does get into your eyes, simply flush with water.

This recipe utilizes the trick of blending flower petals with bottled aloe vera gel to extract their color and benefits, without the risk of early spoilage a simple rose water infusion would carry. It should keep well in your refrigerator for 1 month, or longer.

Chamomile Calming Syrup

This tasty syrup contains chamomile, a gentle herb that calms, relaxes and helps you unwind from a busy day. A touch of lemon balm is added, for its ability to smooth frayed nerves and quiet the mind. Raw honey is a sweet-tasting product that acts as a preservative in this syrup.

YIELD: 4 OUNCES (120 ML)

3 to 4 fresh or dried lemon balm leaves

1 tbsp (1 g) dried chamomile flowers or tea

¼ cup (60 ml) simmering hot water

¼ cup (60 ml) raw honey

Few drops of peppermint extract (optional)

Tear or crumble the lemon balm leaves into small pieces, then add them to a heatproof mug or jar along with the chamomile flowers. Pour the hot water over them and allow to steep for 45 minutes.

Strain and stir in the raw honey until dissolved. Add a few drops of peppermint extract for flavor, if you'd like.

Take 1 to 2 teaspoons (5 to 10 ml) several times a day, or as needed. You can also add it to a cup of hot tea. This syrup is especially good to take in the evening to promote a more restful sleep.

Store the finished syrup in your refrigerator. Shelf life is around 4 weeks. You can also freeze small amounts in ice cube trays for up to 6 months and thaw at room temperature, when needed.

While both herbs are generally safe for most people, if you have health conditions, severe allergies or are pregnant or nursing, check with a health care provider before taking medicinal amounts of any herbs. Honey-containing products should not be given to children under the age of 1.

Tip: If you're allergic to chamomile, try making this syrup with more lemon balm. Peppermint extract can be found in the baking and spice section of your local grocery store and is not to be confused with the much more potent peppermint essential oil.

Nontoxic Solutions for the Home

In this chapter, you'll learn how to ditch the store-bought toxins and their health-damaging side effects and make your own simple but effective household cleaners, using just a few inexpensive ingredients from the grocery store, along with flowers and herbs from the garden.

These are great projects for using your more aromatic and antibacterial herbs, such as rosemary, sage, thyme and oregano. Roses and lavender add a soft and subtle scent to some of the recipes, but if you're not a fan of floral, try using citrus-scented herbs or zest in their place.

Make chore time safe for your kids by mixing together an all-natural lemon-scented dusting spray that contains no endocrine disruptors or persistent chemicals that will damage their long-term health, unlike the canned dusting sprays that line store shelves.

Skip the commercial disinfectant wipes, which are linked to respiratory and immune issues, and brew up an herbal vinegar spray that has legendary disinfecting properties and is perfect for cleaning your home during cold and flu season.

Instead of spraying your windows with strongly scented blue sprays that can cause respiratory problems and skin irritation, try my pretty rose window cleaner for a streak-free shine that won't harm you, your family or the environment.

I also share recipes to naturally clean your laundry, counters, floors and more!

Thyme Counter Cleaner

This recipe makes cleaning your counters a breeze! Castile soap lifts dirt and grime, while the water helps rinse it away. Germ-busting thyme is infused into common isopropyl (rubbing) alcohol, which helps the spray dry to a non-streak shine. If you're sensitive to the scent of rubbing alcohol, try using clear vodka instead.

YIELD: 1 CUP (250 ML)

1 tbsp (1 g) dried thyme

3 tbsp (45 ml) isopropyl (rubbing) alcohol

1 cup (250 ml) water

2 tsp (10 ml) liquid castile soap

FOR THE THYME-INFUSED ALCOHOL

Place the thyme leaves in a small cup or jar and pour the alcohol over them. Cover, and infuse overnight. The alcohol will turn a pretty shade of green. Strain.

FOR THE COUNTER CLEANER

Fill a spray bottle or jar with the water, then gently stir in the castile soap. Pour the infused alcohol into the mixture and stir once more.

Be sure to label your counter cleaner, so no one mistakenly thinks it's an herbal mixture that can be ingested, and keep it out of the reach of small children.

Shake gently before each use. Spritz over your counters, paying extra attention to especially dirty spots. Use a rag or paper towel to wipe and buff dry.

Lemon Thyme Dusting Spray

Those lemon-scented dusting sprays found in your local store's cleaning section may smell nice, but a quick glance at their labels shows products that are far from natural. Instead, try this simple and inexpensive recipe that's healthier for you and your furniture. The vinegar's purpose is to clean and cut through built-up grime, while the olive oil helps protect wood and leaves a nice shine behind. This spray can even help restore and improve the appearance of worn wooden surfaces! I chose lemon thyme for this recipe because it adds a disinfecting boost as it cleans, but you can mix and match whatever variety of lemon-scented herbs you like, such as lemon balm, lemon verbena, lemon thyme and lemongrass.

YIELD: 3 OUNCES (90 ML) DUSTING SPRAY

1 lemon

1 cup (10 g) chopped fresh lemon thyme or other lemon-scented herbs

1 1/2 cups (375 ml) white vinegar

2 tbsp (30 ml) olive oil

Tip: If fresh herbs aren't available, you can use 1/2 cup dried instead.

FOR THE LEMON THYME VINEGAR

Remove the peel from the lemon and cut it into several pieces, or use a grater or zester. Try to get mostly colored zest, avoiding as much white pith as possible.

Place the lemon-scented herbs, pieces of lemon peel and white vinegar in a pint (500-ml) canning jar. Cover with a plastic lid. If you don't have a nonmetallic lid, place a few layers of wax paper or plastic wrap between the lid and jar, to keep the vinegar from corroding the metal.

Set the jar aside in a cupboard or other dark place for 1 to 2 weeks or until the vinegar smells distinctly of lemon. If needed, add more lemon peels and infuse a few weeks longer for a stronger scent. After sufficient time has passed, strain the vinegar into a clean jar. Label, cap and store out of sunlight.

The infused vinegar should stay fresh for around a year and can be used to make around 6 batches of dusting spray.

FOR THE DUSTING SPRAY

Combine 4 tablespoons (60 ml) lemon herb vinegar with the olive oil in a small glass spray bottle. Shake well before and during each use, as the mixture tends to separate easily.

Spritz a small amount on a dusting rag and rub over dusty or worn wooden surfaces until they shine and the oil is evenly worked in. This spray can be used on furniture, tables, cabinet doors and other wooden surfaces, but isn't designed for hardwood floors.

Basic Toilet Bowl Cleaner

This simple recipe is effective for routine toilet cleaning. For tougher jobs, try adding ¼ cup (65 g) super washing soda with the baking soda and use a pumice stone to scrub away persistent hard-water stains.

YIELD: ENOUGH TO CLEAN 1 TOILET

½ cup (112 g) baking soda

½ cup (125 ml) Four Thieves Vinegar (page 220)

Sprinkle the baking soda onto the sides and in the bowl of your toilet. Next, pour in the vinegar. It should immediately start bubbling up and fizzing. If not, try using ¾ to 1 cup each of baking soda and vinegar next time.

Using a toilet brush, scrub the bowl thoroughly, then flush.

Tip: Use a cotton ball moistened with hydrogen peroxide for lightening stains on and around the toilet lid.

Lemon Balm Furniture Polish

While you can rub your furniture directly with lemon balm leaves for a fresh scent and shine, it takes a lot of leaves, time and patience to do so. Instead, try drying your lemon balm leaves and infusing them into an oil that has a long shelf life, such as jojoba, coconut or olive, then turn that into a homemade polish that makes your wooden surfaces gleam!

YIELD: 1 OUNCE (28 G)

1 tbsp (1 g) dried lemon balm leaves, crumbled

1 oz (30 ml) jojoba oil

0.15 oz (4 g) beeswax

Lemon essential oil, optional

Place the dried lemon balm leaves and jojoba oil in a half-pint (250-ml) canning jar. Set the jar down into a saucepan containing 1 to 2 inches (2.5 to 5 cm) of water. Heat over a burner set to low for 1 hour, then strain oil into a 4-ounce (125-ml) canning jar. You can save a little bit of cleanup time by using this small jar for both mixing together and storing the furniture polish.

Weigh out the beeswax directly into the jar with the strained oil, then set it in the saucepan you used to infuse the jojoba oil. Turn the heat to medium-low and heat until the beeswax is completely melted. Remove from heat. If desired, stir in a few drops of lemon essential oil, for scent and added cleaning power.

Using scraps of old T-shirts or other soft rags, rub a small amount into your wooden furniture, rolling pins and cutting boards as needed. Follow with a buffing by a clean rag.

Rose Window Cleaner

Brighten up chore time with this pretty pink window cleaner made from fresh roses. It utilizes the natural grease- and grime-cutting abilities of white vinegar. Cornstarch may sound like an odd ingredient, but its specific purpose in the recipe is to help prevent streaking. For the most beautiful, streak-free shine, try using this spray in conjunction with crumpled newspaper or birdseye cotton (the material that diaper flats are made of).

YIELD: ENOUGH TO FILL A 2-OUNCE (60-ML) SPRAY BOTTLE

1 cup (10 g) fresh pink or red rose petals

1½ cups (375 ml) white vinegar

2 tbsp (30 ml) water

Pinch of cornstarch

FOR THE ROSE-INFUSED VINEGAR

Place the rose petals and vinegar in a pint (500-ml) canning jar. Cover with a plastic or nonmetallic lid. If you don't have one, place a few layers of plastic wrap or wax paper over the jar before putting the lid on, to keep the vinegar from corroding the metal.

Set the jar aside in a cool, dark place for 1 to 2 weeks or until the vinegar turns pink and takes on a light rose scent. If you'd like a stronger smell, add more rose petals and infuse for another week. Strain the finished vinegar into a clean jar. Label, cap and store out of direct sunlight. The color will fade over time, but the vinegar will remain usable for at least 1 year, or longer.

FOR THE ROSE WINDOW CLEANER

Pour 2 tablespoons (30 ml) of rose-infused vinegar into a small spray bottle. Add the water and cornstarch and shake well.

Spritz on windows, mirrors and other glass surfaces, then wipe off with crumpled newspaper or birdseye cotton. Vinegar can damage or cause etching on granite, stone or marble, so avoid using on those types of surfaces.

Tip: It's easy to scale this recipe up to make larger quantities. Just combine equal parts of water and vinegar, plus a pinch of cornstarch.

Four Thieves Vinegar Spray

There is an old legend of four thieves who went around robbing the homes and graves of those who had been stricken by the plague during medieval times. The mystery of why they never got sick themselves was solved when they were finally captured and gave up their secret in exchange for pardons of their crimes. They claimed to have steeped a special blend of herbs in vinegar, then soaked rags in it to cover their faces and to wash with during and after their nefarious acts. Whether such a band of thieves actually existed or not may never be known, but scientific research today tells us that many aromatic herbs do indeed have strong disinfecting and antimicrobial properties. I like to make up a large batch of this vinegar each year to keep on hand for use during cold and flu season. It's great for cleaning surfaces such as sinks, light switches, toilet seats, refrigerator handles and other places germs might lurk. While there may have been only four thieves in the legend, you're not limited to using just four herbs in this recipe. The original formulas that sprang up around that time were thought to contain many herbs, for the widest array of benefits possible.

YIELD: 1½ CUPS (375 ML)

¼ cup (3 to 4 g) each of chopped fresh rosemary, mint, lavender leaves, sage, thyme and oregano

Few whole cloves (optional)

1½ cups (375 ml) vinegar

Water, for diluting

Place the herbs in a pint (500-ml) canning jar. Some variations of the recipe contain cloves, for their potent germ-fighting properties. If you like their scent, try adding a few to the jar. Pour the vinegar over the herbs. Add extra vinegar, if needed, to ensure that the herbs are fully covered.

Cover with a nonmetallic lid or place a few layers of wax paper or plastic wrap between the jar and metal lid, to prevent corrosion from the vinegar.

Set the vinegar in a dark place to infuse for 1 to 2 weeks. Strain and store in a glass jar. Shelf life is at least one year.

To use, dilute with equal parts of water, and spray on soiled or germy areas, then wipe off with old rags or paper towels. Vinegar can damage or cause etching on granite, stone or marble, so avoid using on those types of surfaces.

Tip: If you don't have fresh herbs, try using half as much dried herb instead.

Orange Pine Floor Cleaner

The grime-fighting powers of citrus combine with the disinfecting woodsy scent of pine in this basic floor cleaner recipe for no-wax and ceramic tile flooring. Avoid using on hardwood floors, since the acid in vinegar may damage finishes over time.

YIELD: 1^1/$_2$ CUPS (375 ML) FLOOR CLEANER

^{1}/$_2$ cup (12 g) chopped pine needles

Zest or peelings from 1 orange

1^1/$_2$ (375 ml) cups white vinegar

Place the pine needles and orange zest in a pint (500-ml) jar. It doesn't matter if you have a large or small orange; there's no precise amount needed for this recipe.

Pour the vinegar into the jar. Add extra, if needed, to cover all of the plant material. Cap with a nonmetallic lid. If one isn't available, place a few layers of plastic wrap or wax paper between the jar and lid, to prevent corrosion from the vinegar.

Tuck the vinegar away in a dark cupboard for 1 to 2 weeks, then strain.

If you'd like a stronger scent, fill a new jar with a fresh supply of pine needles and orange peel and pour the freshly strained vinegar on top. Repeat the 1- to 2-week waiting time to create a double-strength infusion.

To use, mix ^{1}/$_4$ to ^{1}/$_2$ cup (60 to 120 ml) orange pine floor cleaner into a gallon (3.8 L) of hot water and mop as usual.

Herbal Hand Soap

Sometimes, it's more convenient to use a liquid soap, rather than a bar, for washing hands. Some people, too, prefer the feel of liquid soap to solid bars. For those situations, it's a breeze to mix up a natural solution that doesn't contain all of the synthetic detergents and heavy fragrances that store-bought hand soaps tend to have. For best results with this recipe, use a handmade or real soap, such as castile, since many store-bought bars are actually detergent based and won't work as well. This project is also a great way to use up odd-size ends and scraps of the handmade soaps found in the Simple Homemade Soaps chapter (page 153). Since you only need a small amount, just use a bit of matching or complementary herbal-infused oil from another project, or plain oil that has not been infused.

YIELD: 1½ TO 2 CUPS (375 TO 500 ML)

1 (4- to 5-oz [115- to 145-g]) bar of handmade or other real soap

1 tsp herbal infused oil

1½ to 2 cups (375 to 500 ml) water

Natural preservative (optional)

Using an inexpensive box grater, grate the bar of soap. You should end up with around 1½ to 2 cups (375 to 500 ml) of soap flakes. It's okay if you have a little more or a little less; you can adjust the water to compensate. Place the soap flakes in a medium saucepan, then add the oil and around 1 cup (250 ml) of the water.

Set the pan over a low burner and heat the mixture, occasionally stirring, until the soap flakes dissolve into the water. This will take some time, so don't despair if it doesn't happen quickly.

Add another ½ cup (125 ml) of water and stir. Depending on your initial bar of soap's size and how old it is, you may not need all of the water, or you may need more. As you stir every so often, a layer of foamy bubbles may appear on the surface. You can skim those off carefully with a large spoon or ladle.

Once it's fully dissolved, remove the pan from heat and let the liquid soap cool slightly. Pour into a soap dispenser or bottle. The soap will thicken more as it cools, but should remain in a liquid state. If it doesn't, return it to the saucepan and stir in more water.

Anytime you introduce water into a product, there's an opportunity for bacteria and mold to grow. The alkalinity of soap preserves it in many ways, but if you don't plan on using all of the hand soap within a few weeks, you should consider adding a natural preservative.

Lavender Laundry Detergent

It's so easy to make your own laundry detergent! This project calls for the Coconut Laundry Soap recipe found on page 187. If you're unable to make your own, look for natural laundry soap bars in your local grocery or health store. I like to add a small amount of sweet-scented lavender to my detergent, but you can use another herb, such as lemongrass, instead, or leave the herbs out completely.

YIELD: 16 TO 24 LOADS OF LAUNDRY

1 bar homemade Coconut Laundry Soap (page 187)

1 1/2 to 2 cups (405 to 540 g) super washing soda

1/4 cup (6 g) dried lavender (optional)

1/2 to 1 tsp lavender essential oil (optional)

1/4 to 1/2 cup (60 to 120 ml) Lavender Fabric Softener (page 229) per laundry load (optional)

Using an inexpensive box grater, grate the bar of soap. You should end up with about 1 1/2 cups (75 g) of grated soap.

Place the soap flakes in the bowl of a food processor. Add the super washing soda.

Using an electric coffee grinder or mortar and pestle, pulverize the lavender, then rub it through a fine mesh sieve, so that a fine powder results. This should yield around 1 tablespoon (1 g) of powder. Add the lavender powder to the food processor.

Pulse the soap flakes, super washing soda and lavender powder until it's completely mixed, with no visible flakes of soap remaining. Stir in the lavender essential oil, if using.

Pour into a glass jar, label and close tightly. Use 2 to 3 tablespoons (26 to 39 g) per load of laundry, along with the fabric softener in the fabric softener dispenser, if using. If you don't have any of the Lavender Fabric Softener made up, you can use plain vinegar as a softener.

Tip: Depending on the size and shape of your soap bar, you may end up with more or less grated soap, and the recipe can easily be adapted to accommodate. For every 1/2 cup (25 g) of grated soap, you'll need 1/2 cup (135 g) of super washing soda.

Fresh Mint Wall Wash

The uplifting smell of mint refreshes and energizes, while natural castile soap lifts and washes away the grime and sticky fingerprints that tend to collect on household walls and doors. If you don't have fresh mint, try using half as much dried.

YIELD: 2½ CUPS (625 ML)

1 cup (14 g) fresh mint leaves

1½ cups (375 ml) simmering hot water

1 cup (250 ml) cold water

1 tsp liquid castile soap

Peppermint essential oil (optional)

Place the mint leaves in a heatproof jar or pitcher. Pour the simmering hot water over the leaves. Let this steep for 20 minutes, then strain.

Combine the strained mint tea with the cold water, then gently stir in the castile soap and 1 to 2 drops peppermint essential oil, if using.

Use old rags to dip in the solution and wipe down walls, doors and window frames. Make up only enough wall wash that you can use at once; it doesn't store well beyond 1 day.

Lavender Fabric Softener

Vinegar is one of the most frugal fabric softeners around. It helps to remove leftover detergent and softens your clothing as it does so. While lavender is a favorite at our house because of its tick-repelling properties and sweet scent, try infusing your vinegar with a variety of your favorite flowers, herbs and citrus zest to brighten up your laundry routine.

YIELD: ENOUGH FOR AROUND 6 LOADS OF LAUNDRY

2/3 cup (24 g) dried lavender flowers

1 1/2 cups (375 ml) white vinegar

Combine the lavender flowers and white vinegar in a pint (500-ml) jar. Cap with a nonmetallic lid and let steep for 1 to 2 weeks, out of direct sunlight. If you have only metal lids, place a few sheets of plastic wrap or wax paper between the jar and lid, to prevent corrosion from the vinegar.

Strain the finished vinegar. It will have turned a pretty shade of pink at this point and carry the faint scent of lavender. If you'd like a stronger floral smell, fill a new jar with a fresh supply of dried lavender flowers and pour the freshly strained vinegar on top. Repeat the infusion process for another 1 to 2 weeks, then strain again.

To use, add around 1/4 cup (60 ml) to the fabric softener dispenser on your machine or use a dispenser ball, available in the laundry section of your local supermarket. You may find that you need up to 1/2 cup (125 ml) if you have hard water.

All-Natural Pet Care

Pets can enjoy the benefits of herbs and flowers too! In this chapter we'll make a minty fresh treat to help banish dog breath, along with another tasty, vitamin-rich treat that dogs and cats alike will enjoy.

If your pet is always scratching because of pesky fleas, try making some herbal Flea-Repelling Powder (page 233), or soothe their skin with a quick Itchy Skin Rinse (page 234) after a bath.

I also share the all-purpose first-aid salve recipe that I use on everyone from my goats to my chickens to my dogs. It's great for using on humans too!

Our pets offer companionship, entertainment and unconditional love. For many households, they're also valued members of the family. Why not make them their own natural and nontoxic products too?

Herbal Dry Shampoo or Flea-Repelling Powder

This dry shampoo or powder helps dogs feel and smell fresher between baths. It can also be used as an itch-relieving aid for dogs and cats plagued with irritated skin. Ground lavender flowers are added for their calming, flea-repelling aroma, while neem powder contributes a powerful punch against existing fleas. Both herbs are gentle and safe for cats and dogs in their natural, dried form. Lavender essential oil and neem oil are much stronger, though, and are not suitable substitutes in this recipe.

YIELD: ¼ CUP (40 G) HERBAL DRY SHAMPOO

1 tbsp (1 g) dried lavender flowers

¼ tsp neem leaf powder

¼ cup (40 g) arrowroot powder

Using an electric coffee grinder or mortar and pestle, grind the lavender flowers to a fine powder. Stir together with the neem and arrowroot until a uniform consistency is reached. Do not add any essential oils to this recipe, especially if you plan to use it on cats. Store the finished dry shampoo in a tightly sealed jar.

To use, scoop or pinch up a small amount of powder and rub it into your cat's or dog's fur. Follow with a thorough brushing. Depending on the size of your pet and their cooperation level, this may get messy! Although it's easily vacuumed if it gets in your carpet or on your floor, you may want to apply this outdoors.

Animals and their human handlers who are pregnant or nursing should avoid neem.

Variation: If neem powder isn't available, try finely powdered dried oxeye daisy flowers instead.

Itchy Skin Rinse

This after-bath rinse is designed to help relieve and soothe your dog's itchy skin. Cats don't often require or appreciate bathing, so this recipe wasn't created with them in mind. Dill provides limonene, a compound with flea-killing properties, while calendula, rose and lavender flowers help calm irritation and inflammation. The antiseptic action of yarrow makes it a good addition if your pet has scratched raw spots on their skin. Yarrow may also help repel fleas. While this rinse can offer temporary relief, if your dog has chronic skin issues, you may want to investigate whether something in their diet is the culprit.

YIELD: 2½ CUPS (625 ML)

1½ cups (375 ml) apple cider vinegar

Fresh dill

Calendula flowers

Yarrow

Lavender

Rose petals and leaves

1 cup (250 ml) warm water

Heat the vinegar to a gentle simmer.

Fill a 1-quart (1-L) canning jar halfway with as many of the herbs and flowers that you have on hand. While fresh dill is optimal, it's fine if the other ingredients are dried, if that's what's available to you.

Cover the flowers and herbs with the hot apple cider vinegar. Let cool to a comfortable temperature, then strain into a mixing bowl or pitcher. Add the warm water and pour over your dog as a final rinse after their bath.

All-Purpose Animal Salve

Calendula and plantain speed the healing of cuts, scratches, burns, scrapes, bug bites, hot spots and other minor skin irritations. This salve can be used on dogs, cats, horses, chickens, cows, goats, sheep, pigs and humans too! Because calendula may contain tiny traces of salicylic acid, which cannot be metabolized properly by cats, it should be used sparingly on them, or cat owners may wish to omit calendula from the salve altogether.

YIELD: 5.5 OUNCES (156 G) SALVE

5 oz (150 ml) olive or sunflower oil

¼ cup (2 g) dried calendula flowers

¼ cup (1 g) dried plantain leaves, crumbled

½ oz (14 g) beeswax

Infuse the oil with the calendula flowers and plantain leaves, using one of the methods on page 17.

Combine the infused oil and beeswax in a heatproof canning jar. Place the jar in a saucepan containing a few inches of water. Set the pan over a medium-low burner until the beeswax is melted. Once melted, you can leave the salve in the jar for storage or pour it into small tins.

Apply to pets as needed. Shelf life is around 9 months.

Variation: Try using violet leaves if plantain is not available.

Peppermint & Parsley Fresh-Breath Dog Treat

This cool treat combines fresh peppermint and parsley to help bust the bad-breath germs that often plague our dogs. Be sure to use plain unsweetened yogurt in this recipe, since sugar isn't going to help the situation any. It's important to avoid artificial sweeteners and xylitol as well, since those can be quite toxic to our canine buddies.

YIELD: 12 TO 24 TREATS

1 cup (227 g) plain yogurt

2 tbsp (5 g) chopped parsley

2 tbsp (5 g) chopped fresh mint

1 drop pure peppermint extract (optional)

Blend all of the ingredients together in a small food processor. Divide the mixture evenly between the compartments of an ice cube tray. If you have a small-breed dog, make smaller portions and divide between two trays.

Freeze until solid, then remove from the tray. Store the cubes in a freezer bag and keep frozen until use.

Some dogs might not like the hard texture, but they may like the softness of a treat that's been thawed in the refrigerator for several hours.

If your dog has persistent bad breath, an examination of their diet and a checkup at the vet are probably in order to rule out any underlying health conditions.

Nettle & Coconut Oil Vitamin Treats

These tasty treats feature nettle, which is loaded with vitamins and trace minerals, and coconut oil, for its ability to reduce itchiness and promote healthy skin and shiny coats. They are suitable to give to both dogs and cats. Grass-fed butter is an optional healthy add-in for pets that might not like the taste of straight coconut oil.

YIELD: 12 TO 24 SMALL TREATS

½ cup (100 g) unrefined coconut oil

¼ cup (3 g) dried nettle leaves

4 tbsp (56 g) grass-fed butter (optional)

Infuse the coconut oil with nettles, using the Quick Method on page 17, and then strain.

Pour the strained nettle-infused coconut oil into tiny silicone molds. Plastic ice cub trays can be used for larger dog breeds, and can be filled halfway, so the treats aren't too large.

Place the molds in the refrigerator until they firm up. Remove the treats from the mold and store in a tightly closed jar or container in your refrigerator; they get too soft at room temperature. These make perfect bite-size treats that can be given directly from the refrigerator.

If you have a picky dog who isn't fond of the taste of straight coconut oil, try mixing in ½ tablespoon (7 g) of melted butter per 1 tablespoon (12 g) of coconut oil, and making the treats with that combination instead.

Remember, even though these are healthy treats, you can still overfeed your pets. I give just 1 per day to my miniature dachshund and cats, while my larger-breed dogs get 2 or 3. If your pet has pancreatitis or trouble digesting fats, consult with your veterinarian for their advice.

Resources

While I like to buy local whenever possible, some supplies and ingredients need to be ordered from the Internet. It can be confusing, trying to find reliable and high-quality places to order from, so I've assembled a list of online vendors I've purchased from and have had good experiences with.

ANTIOXIDANTS

Vitamin E and rosemary extract (also called rosemary antioxidant) are two antioxidants that will help your oil-based products, such as salves, lip balms, body butters and lotion bars, last longer. You can buy organic and non-GMO sourced versions from:

Mountain Rose Herbs—http://mountainroseherbs.com

BEESWAX

Support your local beekeeper by buying this locally, if possible. Check the farmer's market and health stores in your area. You can also buy convenient beeswax pastilles at:

Bramble Berry—http://brambleberry.com

Mountain Rose Herbs—http://mountainroseherbs.com

BOTTLES, TINS & JARS

Small 4-ounce (125-ml) glass mason jars from the canning section of my local grocery or feed store make fantastic containers to keep salves, lotions, creams and bath salts in. Tins, cobalt or amber glass jars and glass spray bottles aren't available locally, so I purchase them from the following sites:

Mountain Rose Herbs—http://mountainroseherbs.com

Specialty Bottle—http://specialtybottle.com

CANDELILLA WAX

This vegan wax makes a great substitute for beeswax. Since it has a limited growing area and the potential to be overharvested, consider sunflower wax as another vegan alternative:

Bramble Berry—http://brambleberry.com

COSMETIC CLAY

I love to use naturally colored clays in soaps and face masks. You can find a variety of choices at the follow sites:

Bramble Berry—http://brambleberry.com

Mountain Rose Herbs—http://mountainroseherbs.com

DRIED HERBS & FLOWERS

I enjoy growing as many different types of herbs and flowers as I can, but some years may end up with a smaller harvest than I need. When that happens, I supplement my supply with high-quality dried herbs from these two fine vendors:

Bulk Herb Store—http://bulkherbstore.com

Mountain Rose Herbs—http://mountainroseherbs.com

LIP BALM CONTAINERS & SUPPLIES

Making lip balm is such a fun activity for all ages! It also makes a great last-minute gift and stocking stuffer. You can buy lip balm tubes, pots, printable labels and slider tins at these sites:

Bramble Berry—http://brambleberry.com

Rustic Escentuals—http://rusticescentuals.com

OILS & COSMETIC BUTTERS

While you can buy and use oils from your grocery store, sometimes they're past their prime and may make your products go rancid more quickly. For a wonderful selection of reliably fresh and high-quality oils and butters, try one of the following businesses:

Bramble Berry—http://brambleberry.com

From Nature With Love—http://fromnaturewithlove.com

Majestic Mountain Sage—http://thesage.com

Mountain Rose Herbs—http://mountainroseherbs.com

Nature's Garden—http://naturesgardencandles.com

(continued)

Resources (continued)

PRESERVATIVES

There are several other preservative options at the two sites listed below that you may want to explore. Read descriptions carefully, since some are natural and some are synthetics:

Lotion Crafter—http://lotioncrafter.com

The Herbarie—http://theherbarie.com

SUNFLOWER WAX

This is a pure white, very hard wax processed from sunflowers, making it another great vegan alternative to beeswax:

Nature's Garden—http://naturesgardencandles.com

WEBSITES

Below, I've listed my website, along with several others that you may enjoy reading and learning from.

The Nerdy Farm Wife—This is my site! If you enjoyed the projects in this book, be sure to subscribe to my newsletter so you can get my latest soap-making and herbal-crafting ideas sent to your email each month. http://thenerdyfarmwife.com

The Soap Queen—This site has lots of fun tutorials for soap making and body care products. http://thesoapqueen.com

The Mountain Rose Blog—If you love in-depth and helpful herbal project tutorials with accompanying beautiful photography, you'll love this blog! http://mountainroseblog.com

Bulk Herb Store Blog—This site has more great herbal projects and gorgeous photos. http://www.bulkherbstore.com/blog

HERBAL EDUCATION

The Herbal Academy—I've taken a few online herbal classes from here and they're fantastic. They also have a blog with solidly researched and interesting herbal projects. http://herbalacademyofne.com

Dawn Combs—As an ethnobotanist and author, Dawn offers beginner-level Heal Local™ bootcamps and year-long, long-distance herbal certification programs. http://www.mockingbirdmeadows.com.

The Bellebuono School Of Herbal Medicine—This school offers local or distance certificate programs, lectures and retreats. http://www.hollybellebuono.com

Acknowledgments

This book would not exist without the encouragement and support generously given to me by readers and subscribers of The Nerdy Farm Wife. For much of my life, I never really felt like I fit in anywhere. Now I know, I just needed to make my own place in the world, where I could visit with a flow of like-minded friends on a regular basis. I love and adore my blog readers because they are simply the best!

Thank you to Will Kiester and the entire Page Street team, for providing the opportunity to write the book that was in my heart. Page Street invests a tremendous amount of time and care into the books they publish, and I'm so honored to be included in their lineup.

To Sarah, my editor at Page Street, goes an added dose of thanks. She took my terribly rough manuscript and helped polish it into a work to be proud of. I'm a slow writer that can't always easily find the right words I want to say, so I really appreciate her kind patience while working with me!

Special thanks goes to my daughter, for her helpful artistic opinions and delicious homemade snacks that kept my brain and tummy fueled, and to my son, for voluntarily taking over laundry duty this year and being my go-to guy for fixing and toting stuff. You're the best kids around and I'm proud to be your mom!

Much love and appreciation goes to my sweet and ever-supportive husband, for always believing in me and working so hard to give our family the peaceful life it has. I look forward to many more years of our never-boring, farm-life adventures!

Thank you, to my parents, for raising me in a happy, loving home where I had the freedom to follow my own interests. I appreciate all of the hard work and sacrifices it took to make that happen!

To my mother and father-in-law who are always so good to our family, I appreciate the support and the yummy gluten-free food sent our way, when deadlines and crunch times came around!

To Grandpa Al, who would come over to look at my garden, quietly chuckle and then patiently help me fix whatever I had managed to mess up that time—eternal thanks for making our life so much better, in so many ways. Thankfully, green thumbs can be taught and mine came from him. Not a day goes by that we don't think about or miss Grandpa Al.

To my friend Kay Taylor, who is one of the nicest people on earth. She allowed me to share her wonderful deodorant recipe with you (page 195), plus gifted me with the gorgeous peonies that inspired the idea for Peony Orange Scrub (page 115).

A big shout-out goes to my friend Kyle "Q" Gordon, who took time from his busy life to write up a long list of fun things I could do while recuperating from an unhealthy online video game addiction. Without his encouragement and our (still-unfinished) bucket list challenge, the thought of starting a blog probably would've never crossed my mind.

Last, but certainly not least, a special thank you to my creative, talented brothers, sisters and other family members who I'm lucky to be related to. Friends sometimes come and go, but family is forever!

About the Author

Jan Berry lives on a farm in the Blue Ridge Mountains of Virginia with her handsome husband and two homeschooled kids, along with a menagerie of chickens, goats, turkeys, pigs, ducks, rabbits, bees and dogs, plus one rascally cat.

She enjoys brainstorming creative ways to turn herbs, flowers and weeds into pretty things, that are fun and practical to use. In 2013, she founded her blog, The Nerdy Farm Wife, so she could share those ideas with the world at large.

When she's not trying to convert every citizen of the world into a dandelion-lover, she enjoys playing word games, eating gluten-free pizza, reading and enjoying life with her family.

Index